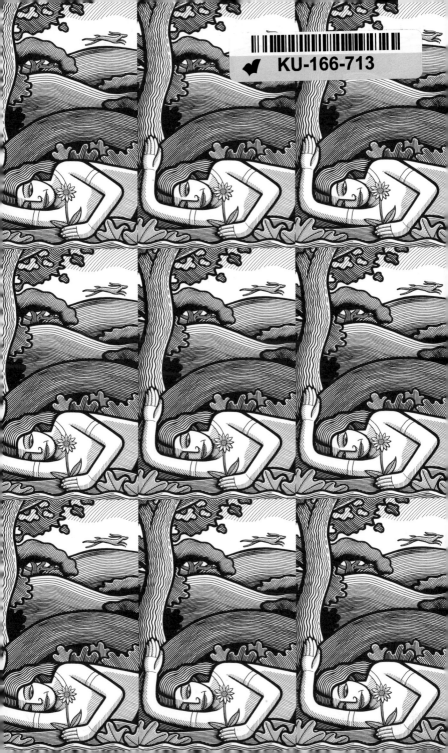

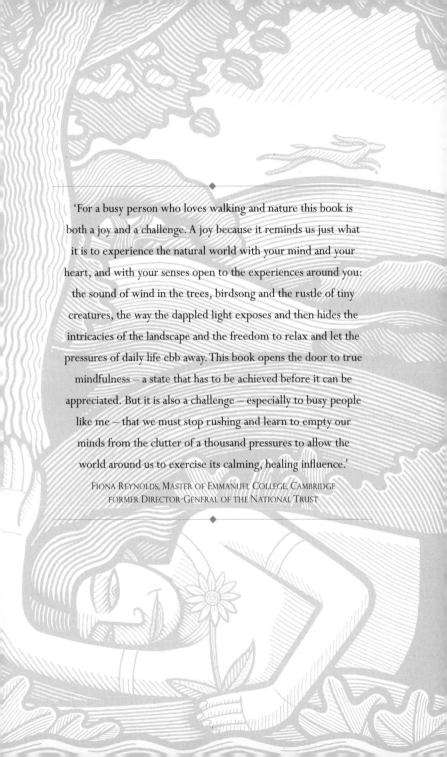

'For a busy person who loves walking and nature this book is both a joy and a challenge. A joy because it reminds us just what it is to experience the natural world with your mind and your heart, and with your senses open to the experiences around you: the sound of wind in the trees, birdsong and the rustle of tiny creatures, the way the dappled light exposes and then hides the intricacies of the landscape and the freedom to relax and let the pressures of daily life ebb away. This book opens the door to true mindfulness – a state that has to be achieved before it can be appreciated. But it is also a challenge – especially to busy people like me – that we must stop rushing and learn to empty our minds from the clutter of a thousand pressures to allow the world around us to exercise its calming, healing influence.'

FIONA REYNOLDS, MASTER OF EMMANUEL COLLEGE, CAMBRIDGE
FORMER DIRECTOR-GENERAL OF THE NATIONAL TRUST

Mindfulness
& the Natural
World

Bringing Our Awareness Back to Nature

Claire Thompson

Leaping Hare Press

First published in the UK in 2013 by

Leaping Hare Press

210 High Street, Lewes
East Sussex BN7 2NS, UK
www.leapingharepress.co.uk

British Library Cataloguing-in-Publication Data
A catalogue record for this book is available from
the British Library

ISBN: 978-1-78240-102-5

This book was conceived, designed and produced by

Leaping Hare Press

Creative Director PETER BRIDGEWATER
Publisher SUSAN KELLY
Commissioning Editor MONICA PERDONI
Editorial Director TOM KITCH
Art Director JAMES LAWRENCE
Editor JENNI DAVIS
Designer GINNY ZEAL
Illustrator CLIFFORD HARPER

Printed in China
Colour origination by Ivy Press Reprographics
Distributed worldwide (except North America) by
Thames & Hudson Ltd., 181A High Holborn,
London WC1V 7QX, United Kingdom

5 7 9 10 8 6 4

CONTENTS

INTRODUCTION

*We all have one thing in common: we are
part of the natural world. No matter what our
nationality is, what we do for a living, what our
interests or beliefs are, we share the same natural home.
How would we be here enjoying our everyday lives,
if it weren't for our bodies, the trees, the sun in the
sky and the air we are breathing? The simple answer
is that we wouldn't. Nature gives rise to all of life
on the planet, including our own, and connecting
with the natural world is an integral part of our
happiness and well-being.*

DISCOVERING MINDFULNESS IN NATURE

◆

One of the greatest problems we face in our lives today is that, somewhere along the way, we have forgotten that we are all part of nature. Since the human race evolved hundreds of thousands of years ago, we have gradually separated ourselves from the natural world. In fact, our modern everyday lives often involve very little contact with nature at all.

W<small>HY IS THIS IMPORTANT?</small> Because it has led us to deprive ourselves of the simple of joy of living, with harmful consequences for our own happiness and well-being, as well as for the well-being of the rest of life on Earth.

This book is an invitation on a journey to explore the innate bond we all have with the natural world, and to discover the infinite happiness and freedom that lies in the simple experience of being alive. Nature is around us and within us wherever we are and whatever is going on in our lives. You don't need to know anything about animals, plants, biology or the environment to enjoy the wonder of the natural world.

I hope to lead you on a path to discover the fulfilling enjoyment, calm, vitality and companionship to be found in nature. How can you do this? All you need is your body, an open mind and a little touch of nature in your life. This is where mindfulness comes in.

We have forgotten that we are part of nature.

What Is Mindfulness?

Mindfulness is simply about being aware of our experience of the present moment of our lives. Do you ever feel you spend a lot of your time distracted by your mind worrying about the past, planning for the future or criticizing yourself? Mindfulness is about realizing that, instead, there is happiness in accepting and letting go of these distractions. It is about paying attention and noticing the life within us and in the natural world around us, here and now. Mindfulness will enable you to let happiness into your life along the way, by engaging with your experience more fully. If you are new to mindfulness, be kind and patient with yourself in your exploration of it. It is an enjoyable journey of continuous discovery that requires time and practice.

Mindfulness and the Natural World

As our awareness of the natural world grows, we begin to notice that the separation we have created between ourselves and nature starts to fade and realize that our well-being is intimately interlinked with the well-being of the rest of the natural world. We begin to feel a sense of reverence and affection for all of nature and to understand that we are an integral part of something much larger than ourselves: the web of life.

Mindfulness of the natural world becomes an essential practice in the context of the current destruction we are inflicting upon our planet. As we become more aware of our experience of nature, and develop a true love for the natural world, we are more likely to start to take positive action to protect our universal home.

A Passion for Nature

I have a passion for the natural world. Spending time in nature fills me with happiness, wonder, calm, comfort and strength. It gifts me with a sense of belonging and brings me closer to who I really am. Its infinite beauty, mystery and complexity never cease to amaze me. The natural world is an endless source of discovery that is free and accessible to us at all times. My personal belief is that if we pay attention to nature, we can fall under its spell, no matter who we are. Whether we delight in awe-inspiring landscapes, enjoy the thrill of extreme outdoor sports or quietly retreat to the hills for solitary walks, there is something for us all to enjoy in the natural world.

◆

I wandered lonely as a cloud

That floats on high o'er vales and hills,

When all at once I saw a crowd,

A host, of golden daffodils;

Beside the lake, beneath the trees,

Fluttering and dancing in the breeze.

'DAFFODILS', WILLIAM WORDSWORTH (1770–1850)
ENGLISH ROMANTIC POET

◆

As you read this book, you may learn about yourself, you may learn about others and you may discover things about the rest of life with which you share the planet. However, embark on this journey with no expectations. Above all, it is simply about appreciating nature with a playful sense of childlike wonder. My hope is that by the time you turn the last page you are left with a desire to sit under trees, roll around in sand dunes, follow streams, climb to the top of mountains, seek out beautiful views and marvel at intimate encounters with other animals and plants. Accept this invitation with openness and curiosity, enjoying whatever you experience along the way.

CHAPTER ONE

WE ARE NATURE

Nature and people are simply part of one another. If we bring our awareness to what is around us and within us, this becomes obvious. We cannot be considered separate. The natural world is at the very heart of our being. If we are willing to listen and pay attention to nature, we will begin to recognize our innate sense of connection and belonging. Mindfulness of the natural world is likely to be one of our deepest experiences and our greatest opportunities to feel truly alive.

WE ARE LIFE ITSELF!

❖

We are alive. Along with every other living being on our planet, we have been gifted the simple yet wondrous opportunity to embody life. What if the point of our lives were simply to live among all the beautiful life forms that have arisen in the natural world?

CONSIDER FOR A MOMENT that the joy of being alive could be our only purpose. We belong in the natural world. We are the natural world, just like the trees, the flowers, the sun and the sky.

When I am out in nature, I feel an innate sense of belonging. I don't feel alone, I feel alive. Experiencing the mystery of a forest, noticing the sunlight flicker on a tree's leaves, watching the flow of a stream trickling over rocks or listening to the song of a bird, I always find companionship in nature. We are not separate. We are integral parts of each other.

As human beings with the ability for conscious thought, it is easy to live our lives wrapped up in our problems, dwelling on the past, planning for the future, caught up in urges of obtaining pleasure and trying to rid ourselves of pain. What if we stopped for a moment and opened up to life as it is right now, in front of us? Live in it. Listen to it, look at it, smell it, touch it and taste it, as often as you can. Feel the simple experience of being alive. It is always accessible, wherever we are, whatever we are doing and whatever is going on in our lives.

Have you ever just sat down for a moment and felt the warmth of the sun on your face? Appreciated some beautiful flowers in a park on your way to the supermarket? Or marvelled at stunning displays of autumn colours in the trees? Try it. Notice nature around you. Give it your full attention from time to time. Experience it with all your senses, and really *look*, as if you are encountering it for the first time. You too are nature. You too are alive.

MINDFULNESS PRACTICE

IN TOUCH WITH THE EARTH

When we are in touch with the earth, we can appreciate that we are part of all that is around us. Find some grass, a meadow, a park or a bit of garden where you won't be disturbed. Lie down on the ground. Become aware of the earth beneath you. Close your eyes and become aware of your breath. Notice what your breathing is like. Bring your attention to how each part of your body feels as it is in contact with the ground. Feel the warmth of the sun on your face, breathe in the scents, notice the breeze against your skin and hear the sounds of nature. Allow yourself to experience this moment and gradually let go of the idea that you are separate — you are connected to the earth and part of life itself.

FINDING MEANING IN THE NATURAL WORLD

If you ever have days when you wonder what life is all about, try this. Sit beneath a big tree, lean back against its trunk and look up through its branches to the sky. Try to put aside for a moment any thoughts you are having at the time and just enjoy being there.

DISCOVERING THAT NATURE IS OUR HOME is the most comforting realization I have ever had. Awareness of the natural world brought meaning and happiness into my life. Every day, regardless of what is going on in my life, the natural world gives me the chance to see that I can enjoy being alive at every moment. We can simply look at nature, listen to it, touch it and smell it. There is always an opportunity to marvel at a beautiful flower, to gain a sense of calm from a breeze, or to watch a bird soaring above us in the sky. When I spend time with nature, I feel an infinite sense of freedom. I can just be myself, as I am in that moment, without being judged.

Many people who have a deep love of nature will tell you that they spent their childhood climbing trees, looking for nature's treasures in the form of beautiful shells and colourful feathers, catching creepy crawlies or sitting outside in their garden listening to the birdsong. The more creative ones enjoyed experimenting with nature, making little boats out of large leaves or putting together daisy chains.

*Try to put aside any thoughts you
are having and just enjoy being there.*

I was not one of those children who spent all their time
exploring the natural world. My true passion for the natural
world dawned upon me much later on, and it was my constant search for meaning and purpose that led me to begin to
connect with the natural world and appreciate it.

Looking for a Purpose

As a child and teenager, I spent much of my time lost in my
mind, riding the roller coaster of my thoughts, which often
led me to feel lonely, trapped and isolated. At school, we are
taught that in order to solve problems we need to analyse
them logically and find a solution; education in our modern
world is largely focused on learning facts, categorizing ideas
and concepts, demonstrating ability to analyse, and finding
answers and explanations to problems. So I believed that if I
analysed and understood everything I was thinking or feeling,
I would be able to control my states of mind and feel happier.

Of course, analysis works in certain situations, such as
solving a mathematical equation, understanding the complex
processes in the development of an embryo, or critically
reviewing a piece of literature. Our thoughts are very good at
helping us to understand and solve problems. However, in
terms of finding a meaning to our lives, I have found that log-

ical thought never got me anywhere. I often found myself thinking for hours on end, attempting to work out a purpose for my life. I wanted to do something worthwhile, yet I couldn't identify meaning anywhere.

Of course, I enjoyed all the things that teenagers like to do. I liked going to the cinema, buying nice clothes, watching television, reading books, going to concerts and spending time with my friends. However, I was constantly searching for a greater meaning to my existence beyond these fun distractions. I read a lot about philosophy and religion and listened to others telling me that the meaning of life was just to get on with daily chores, go to university, have a good career, earn a lot of money, buy a large house and have a family. I struggled to accept any of these pursuits. I just kept thinking to myself, 'Why?' I couldn't see any of them satisfying my desire to find a true purpose.

We Are All Related to Everything!

The only subject I was taught at school that began to reveal some form of meaning was biology. To me, biology was the study of reality and I hoped that it might reveal why I was on this planet. It was an insight into something we can see and observe right in front of us. It was the understanding of ourselves, what is around us and where we come from. Biology is the study of life and living organisms. And, more than anything, I wanted to know about life.

The more I understood and learnt about biology, the more I found it fascinating. I was captivated by the understanding of how our bodies work. I found the process of conception, birth and development mind-blowing. I loved looking at how embryos develop under the microscope and understanding why animals behave the way they do. I enjoyed finding out about the secret lives of plants and how they sustain all life on Earth. I was amazed by the ability that animals, plants, bacteria and other creatures have to adapt to where they live, and by the ways in which all living things consume and transform energy to stay alive.

Amongst everything I discovered, the most comforting, exciting and life-changing fact was that all living things on Earth are related. We are all part of the one great family of life. From the tiniest bacteria, to the trees in the forest, to the birds in my garden, to the elephants on the African plains, we are all connected. This continues to amaze me every time I think about it.

To me, this meant that none of us are alone after all. The natural world is something real that we can see, hear, smell, touch and taste, that we can depend on for companionship. It was my first step towards understanding our innate connection to the natural world. For the first time, I began looking at nature all around me and thinking to myself: 'I am connected to you. I am part of your family.' This comforted me and calmed my questioning thoughts. However, questioning thoughts are usually only temporarily satisfied. They will always find further questions, further problems to solve. And mine continued to search for answers: 'OK, so I am part of the natural world – but what is my role here? What is my meaning here?' This is where mindfulness came in.

WHAT IS MINDFULNESS?

◆

Mindfulness is something we simply do. It is not a theory, or a thought, or a concept. Defined in a few words, mindfulness is paying attention, without judgement and with acceptance, to where we are, how we are, what we are feeling, what we are thinking – in the present moment.

To DISCOVER WHAT MINDFULNESS IS, we need to put it into practice. A key word we can repeat to ourselves at all times when practising mindfulness is 'notice'. Just keep noticing, openly, without trying to change anything, without judgement, without expectation, as often as possible. Notice what you are thinking. Notice what your body feels like. Notice what emotions you are feeling. Notice where you are and what is around you. Notice what you can see, hear, smell, touch or taste. Just notice without seeking to change anything.

Mindfulness is something we simply do. It is not a theory, or a thought, or a concept.

Awakening to Life in an Instant

Mindfulness of the natural world brought me back to myself and, quite simply, to life. My biology lessons had led me to understand my place in the natural world through abstract science. My first true awakening came a few years later, when I was least expecting it. My questioning thoughts had absolutely no role whatsoever to play here. In fact, I wasn't seeking anything. This was the moment when I first fell in love with the natural world. For this, we need to take a short trip to the wilderness of Chile, South America.

I visited the Chilean Lake District when I was eighteen years old, and it was the most beautiful place I had ever seen. Huerquehue National Park, with its stunning views across pristine forests of monkey-puzzle trees, its vast serene lakes shimmering in the sunshine and its snow-capped volcanoes standing majestically in the distance, will always remain a very special place to me.

The Simple Joy of Just Being

I saw the park for the first time on a sunny summer morning in December. After an early-morning climb along a steep, winding path, I reached the park entrance just as the sun was rising over the distant Villarrica volcano. The view was breathtaking. As I entered the park I was surrounded by enormous ancient trees, each delicately draped in lichens, giving the forests a fairy-tale feel. Walking further into the park, I came

---

I felt my lungs inflate with the onrush of

scenery – air, mountains, trees, people. I thought,

'This is what it is to be happy.'

FROM 'THE BELL JAR', SYLVIA PLATH
HEINEMANN, LONDON, 1963

---

across a stunning emerald-green lake. As I stood there, looked and listened for a moment, I noticed the feeling of my feet touching the ground. I heard the melodious song of a bird in the understorey. I sensed the stillness and vastness of the lake. I connected with the peace and silence all around me. I took a deep breath of pure, fresh air. I felt grounded and anchored. As I let my senses continue to take in my surroundings, I experienced a feeling of what can only be described as sacredness. I do not use the word in a religious sense. Rather, I felt an immediate sense of great respect, of being part of something intangible and much greater than myself right there, in that moment. This feeling contained a mix of peace, connectedness, undeniable beauty and a strong sense of reality. I had, for a short moment, completely tuned in to nature.

And it all came to me in that instant, that wordless and thoughtless instant. This is why I was alive. This was the simple joy of just being. My thoughts stopped seeking answers. This fleeting and indecipherable quiver within me was undeniably real. This was where I belonged and I had found my purpose.

WE ARE THE SAME

◆

Consider this. All plants, animals and minerals are nature. They do not separate themselves from one another. They simply co-exist. We are the same. We are an integral part of the natural world. Yet our conscious mind seems to perceive us as separate.

INTERESTINGLY, THERE IS NO SIMPLE DEFINITION of what is meant by the word 'nature'. However, the word is used in many cultures to describe the world without human beings. It often refers to anything that has not been touched or created by humans. This simple definition reveals that our perception of nature is that of the natural world being 'out there', and us being apart from it. However, if we bring our awareness to the world around us, we soon notice that this is not the case.

Since my experience in Chile, feeling part of the natural world is something I have experienced more and more often. I remember once sitting by a small lake surrounded by rocky hillsides and steep mountains. The stillness of the lake, the sound of the water gently splashing up against the rock and the silence that only exists up in the hills filled me with a stable sense of calm. It wasn't the comforting calm you get from receiving a hug from a close friend or snuggling up in your duvet. It was a calm I could never have sought or created myself. It was a larger sense of calm, of which I became an integral part.

Nature Comes Together to Give Rise to Life

Bring your awareness to your body for a moment. Our bodies are made of the same elements as the rest of the natural world. Our skin, our nails, our hair, our brains, our hearts, our bones are all made of the same substances as those found in trees, meadows, animals, flowers, rocks and soil. Biologists believe that all of life on Earth is made of approximately ninety different natural elements.

Our bodies mainly consist of oxygen, carbon, hydrogen, nitrogen, calcium and phosphorus. Other elements are also present, in smaller quantities – potassium, sulphur, sodium, chlorine and magnesium. All of these elements come together to form the building blocks that constitute our bodies. These building blocks include water, proteins, fats and carbohydrates as well as DNA, which encodes all genetic instructions for the development and functioning of living organisms. The elements that support our existence also support the lives of every other person, animal and plant on the planet.

When a person, animal or plant is born, it is the result of the union of natural elements into life. When we die, these elements separate again and return to the rest of nature. In simple terms, the coming together and the separation of nature's building blocks are the essence of life and death. This suggests that life and death are simply the result of natural elements rearranging themselves. Isn't this a beautiful realization? Our bodies are essentially a gift from the natural

> You didn't come *into* this world; you came *out* of it,
>
> like a wave from the ocean.
>
> ALAN WATTS (1915–73)
> BRITISH PHILOSOPHER & WRITER

world, enabling us to embody life on the planet. Think about this next time you are out for a run, cycling to work, dancing on a night out or even at the gym. Using your body is your opportunity to enjoy the simple pleasure of being alive and to live your purpose of incarnating the natural world.

Nature Flows Through Us

The natural world also flows through us. We take in air, water, food, sounds and sights from the outside world. We also return parts of ourselves to the world. We sweat, breathe out and communicate. This means that not only are we made of natural elements, but that nature is also constantly flowing through us. Our skin connects us to the outside world, rather than separates us from it. And as it flows through us, nature is constantly changing and renewing us at every moment.

One simple illustration of nature flowing through us is the experience of breathing, a simple yet wonderful experience. It keeps us alive. It is a good anchor for us to become aware of when our minds are taking control. Notice your breath for a moment. Notice how the air flows into your body, and out of

MINDFULNESS PRACTICE

SHARING NATURE

Take a moment to think about the idea that nature is flowing through you all the time. Think about everything that is solid within your body. Bring to mind your bones, your muscles, your teeth, your skin and your hair. Consider that they all come from the natural world. They are all made of elements that, before becoming part of your body, were part of the rest of the natural world. And they will all be returned to it sooner or later. Consider that these elements never belonged to you, you are sharing them with the natural world.

Think about the water in the world around us. Water is found in our seas, lakes, glaciers, rivers, streams and clouds. It is also found in our bodies. We have water in our cells, our blood, our saliva, our tears and our sweat. Recognize that we are sharing this water with the rest of nature around us.

Air is all around us – we can feel it against our skin and hear it moving through the leaves of trees. Plants release the oxygen we breathe, and the air we exhale is used again by the plants. We are an integral part of the natural world. Air is continually entering and leaving the body as we breathe in and out – we can't hold on to the air, any more than we can hold on to any of the other elements we share.

We inter-breathe with the rain forests, we drink from
the oceans. They are part of our own body.

THICH NHAT HANH (B. 1926)
VIETNAMESE ZEN BUDDHIST MONK, PEACE ACTIVIST & WRITER

---

your body. Notice where you feel your breath entering and leaving your body. Become aware of how the air you are breathing in and the air you are breathing out is never the same air. However, as it passes through your body, it enables oxygen to be transferred to your blood, which then oxygenates all your organs to ensure their function and keep you alive. Being mindful of our breathing is a simple experience of how we are connected to the natural world. We take in air, we give back air, and we share this air with all other living beings.

As nature flows through us, it is also constantly changing us. At a basic level, our breathing re-oxygenates our body, drinking water rehydrates us, sitting in the sunshine warms us up and the dimming evening light causes us to feel sleepy.

Live with the Sensations

Feeling the natural world flow through us can be a truly exhilarating experience. One of my favourite simple experiences of the natural world is walking along a sandy beach with bare feet. I just love it. Whether it is cold, wet, windy, sunny, it doesn't matter. Try it. Just take your shoes and socks off and walk. Feel the softness of the sand against your feet. Notice whether it is warm or cold, wet or dry. Become aware of any sensations you feel on the soles of your feet. Feel how the ground is pulling you towards it. Notice any other sensations you may experience such as the wind rushing through your hair or the scent of sea salt. You may also notice birds soaring over the crashing waves, keeping their balance in the wind with incredible agility. For a moment, remind yourself that you are an integral part of the scene. Be with it. Try to let go of anything else and live with the sensations. Feel life flow through you and just enjoy that magnificent feeling.

ORIGINATING IN A NATURAL WORLD

The evolution of life on our planet – an adventure that began around 4.5 billion years ago with the formation of the Earth itself – is a long and fascinating story into which we now have a lot of insight, thanks to the work of palaeontologists, archaeologists, anthropologists and geneticists.

THIS UNDERSTANDING OF THE ORIGINS OF LIFE ON EARTH came together back in the nineteenth century. Charles Darwin and Alfred Russell Wallace are the British scientists famously responsible for changing the way we see our natural world, by developing the theory of 'evolution through natural selection'. In 1859, Darwin published *On the Origin of Species*.

The affinities of all the beings of the same class have
sometimes been represented by a great tree … As buds
give rise by growth to fresh buds, and these, if vigorous,
branch out and overtop on all sides many a feebler
branch, so by generation I believe it has been with the
great Tree of Life, which fills with its dead and broken
branches the crust of the earth, and covers the surface
with its ever branching and beautiful ramifications.

FROM 'ON THE ORIGIN OF SPECIES', CHARLES DARWIN
JOHN MURRAY, LONDON, 1859

The theory states that animals and plants best suited to their
natural environment are more likely to survive and repro-
duce, passing on to their young the characteristics that helped
them survive. This means that, gradually, individuals of a species change over time. They become better and better adapted
to the environment they are living in. It is this process that led
to the emergence of a 'great Tree of Life'.

The consequence of Darwin's work was the discovery that
we are in fact simply another animal in the Tree of Life and
that all other plants, animals and bacteria are part of the same
family as us. Every life form on our planet descends from one
single ancestor common to us all, probably some sort of tiny
bacterium. The plants and animals we see on the planet today
are the branches of this family tree that have survived and

continue to thrive in this huge web of life. Our natural family is believed now to comprise more than 8.5 million known species and it is estimated that 86 per cent of the species on our planet have not yet even been described.

The emergence of our human species is an extremely recent event in the evolution of life on our planet. When the first humans came to life, they roamed the African savannah, and staying alive and procreating were their only concerns. Perhaps it is not surprising, then, that we may feel a deep sense of connection and belonging in nature. We have our deepest origins in a natural world.

The Evolution of Our Senses

Ever since the emergence of life on Earth, animals, plants, even the tiniest bacteria have needed to obtain information about the world around them to ensure their best chances of survival. At the most basic level, every living creature will sense if anything comes into direct contact with them and will respond by moving closer or pulling away.

When humans evolved in Africa, we used our senses to obtain information from the natural world and take action to ensure we stayed alive. Having good vision meant we were able to judge how far to throw our spears when hunting other animals for food. It also meant we were able to identify the right fruit and vegetables to eat, and avoid plants we had been taught were poisonous by other members of our tribe. Our hearing heightened our awareness of any dangerous animals potentially lingering close by and our sense of touch enabled us to build shelters, use tools and make fires.

Being part of a tribe was also an important aspect of survival. A person living alone was more vulnerable to other animals or harsh weather conditions. The senses played a key role in being part of a social group. For example, some scientists have observed that, compared to other human-like species around at the same time as us, we had a better sense of smell. This could have been very useful to help us recognize our families and enhance friendship and sexual bonds within our tribe. Hearing was essential once language started to evolve and we needed to communicate with other people in our tribe. Our senses evolved in a natural world, too. They are built to take in the natural world and allow us to interact with our fellow humans and other plants and animals.

We can continue to enjoy our senses today in our everyday lives. Listen, feel, smell and look at nature around you. It is thanks to our senses that we are able to experience life.

The Evolution of Our Minds

One of the key features that evolved in our ancestors, and was different from the majority of the animal world, was an increased brain size. This provided us with a greater capacity for conscious thought, to empathize, be creative, learn from the past, plan for the future and communicate with others.

ENJOYING YOUR NATURAL SENSES

❋

So often when we walk – to work, to the shops, to the train station or with the dog – we are caught up in our thoughts and anxieties and unaware of all that's around us. For just ten minutes of a walk that you do regularly, bring your attention to the experience of walking and become aware of any pleasurable sensations you notice, either in your body and its step-by-step movements or in the natural world around you – sunlight and shadows, the breeze flowing past, the feelings of warmth or cold, the scents in the air, the colours of flowers and trees, the songs of birds, the sounds of insects and other animals. Each time you get distracted by your thoughts, acknowledge this, and gently bring your mind back to your senses. Enjoy the simple pleasure of being alive and part of life all around you.

Thanks to these new characteristics, our ancestors were able to use tools, develop more sophisticated relationships with friends, family and enemies, and find new ways of accessing the best food sources. The increase in brain size is also thought to have supported the development of language, art and culture.

The evolution of these capacities gave rise to what we now call the 'mind'. We will explore our minds in the next chapter as they lie at the heart of changing our relationship with the natural world. The point here is that, like our bodies and our senses, our minds too came from nature and were shaped by living in a natural world.

Our bodies, then, are our home, and our senses allow us to feel, think and connect with life all around us. They are our chance to embody life here and now. Bringing awareness to our experience of our lives in our bodies is the opportunity to be alive, in the present moment. Without the experience of our bodies, we would not be alive.

Isn't This Enough?

Sometimes I look up to the sky at night. I look at the stars and the moon and try to conceive how far away they are and how big our universe is. It always gives me a sense of perspective and reminds me that most of our worries and concerns about our lives are transient and relatively insignificant. In moments like this, when I look at the natural world, I often think to myself: 'Isn't this enough? Isn't sharing and participating in this beautifully mysterious natural world enough?' Nature is our home and if we need to have a purpose at all, why isn't it simply being alive, right now?

CHAPTER TWO

LOSING TOUCH WITH OUR HOME

The natural world has gifted us with the ability to consciously reflect, innovate, organize, plan, create, imagine. In the natural environment we evolved in, this was extremely useful. However, these abilities have gradually disconnected us from our direct experience of the world around us, our natural home. We are nature. So losing touch with nature is losing touch with ourselves — often the reason for our unhappiness. What if the simple key to our happiness were to bring our attention back to our home? To be here and now, participating in life itself?

THE HUMAN MIND: A NATURAL WONDER

Following their evolution in a natural world, our minds have become one of the greatest fascinations and mysteries on our planet. They contain our questions, our desires, our thoughts, our emotions, our memories and our sense of self. Simply, our mind is our ability to be aware of our experience.

THE EVOLUTION OF THE MIND led to the development of of language, culture and art. It has enabled us to paint beautiful pictures in caves, to compose breathtaking symphonies and to capture our endless potential for imagination and creativity in a world of literature. It has also enabled us to embark on great adventures of discovery, such as acquiring a better understanding of our solar system and gaining deep insights into the origins of life. Our minds are wonderful. They enable us to express and share our experiences of the world. In a world where survival in a natural environment is no longer the focus of our lives, our minds offer us the incredible potential to simply connect with the world within us and around us. If only we knew how to pay attention.

So What Is the Mind?

Have you ever noticed the number of thoughts racing through your head during the day? Have you noticed what messages these thoughts contain? For a few minutes, put this book down, close your eyes and just notice any thoughts you are having. What are these thoughts? Notice how you are feeling emotionally. Are you sad or happy? Worried? Stressed? Relaxed? Wishing you were elsewhere, doing something different? This is an example of our direct experience of what we call the mind.

Commonly, when we refer to the mind in our modern world, we refer to the part of us that seems to contain our conscious thoughts, our feelings, experiences and memories. It is the 'I' we perceive constantly assessing our lives, criticizing, judging, understanding, seeking pleasure, feeling insecure, comparing ourselves to others, dwelling on the past and worrying about the future. The mind is usually what we consider to be our 'self'. But what is our 'self'? Is it real? Where does it sit? Is it really what we are? These questions have been the subject of fascination and debate since the beginning of humanity.

Different Views of the Mind

Although we know that our minds evolved in a natural world where survival and procreation were our sole purposes in life, understanding what consciousness is remains a constant journey of endless discovery.

The mind has been perceived in so many different ways across different cultures and religions around the world. Some cultures believe it is a purely human attribute, others

see it as something that other animals and non-living objects also have. For example, a number of so-called animist traditions, including Hindu groups and traditional Native American tribes, see the mind as a spiritual essence found in all natural things. They believe that spirits inhabit the sky, sun, stars, moon, mountains, trees and animals.

In ancient cultures and a number of religions, the mind, usually considered to be a part of the 'soul', is thought to be separate from the body. It is often seen as the immortal essence of a person or a living being. The ancient Greeks believed the soul was a separate substance that animated the bodies of living organisms. The French philosopher René Descartes stated that our minds were completely separate from our bodies and did not follow the rules of nature. He is often remembered and quoted as saying, 'I think, therefore I am'. To him, the act of being able to think rationally was a proof of the existence of a separate self and soul. Christianity usually refers to the soul as the immortal part of human beings that is judged by God and destined to spend the rest of time in Heaven or Hell. Every culture and religion has its own interpretation of this unfathomable natural wonder that we call the mind.

MIND, WHO ARE YOU?

◆

Our minds can feel like our closest allies – and our worst enemies. It is worth getting to know the mind, as we would a new friend. If we begin to show an interest, with kindness and acceptance, we will soon notice that our mind is simply doing its job. If we are better acquainted with it, then we can begin to see it for what it is.

OUR THINKING MINDS are like a constant commentary in our heads. They are always assessing and judging situations, trying to solve problems and making up solutions that will lead us to supposedly better, happier lives. 'I am not good enough', 'I am a failure', 'If I earnt more money in my job, I would be happier', 'Nobody likes me' are some examples of the comments you may hear in your mind. Our minds also make judgements about our own and other people's feelings. Have you ever told yourself, 'I shouldn't feel like this' or thought, 'He really just needs to get a grip'?

Whatever they are telling us, our minds frequently take us away from our experience of our lives in the present moment. We all very often walk to work or to the shops, lost in our thoughts, not noticing anything around us along the way. We tend to fuse with every one of our thoughts and live in the realm of the mind. The mind can separate us from our direct experience of life. But what more to life is there than the experience of it here and now?

You Are Not Your Thoughts

Our minds are constantly seeking our attention, but as we become more aware of our thoughts, we realize that they are just words and stories to which we often don't need to attach much importance. One of the most reassuring things I was told when I was younger was: 'You are not your thoughts. Your thoughts are not true.' Many of the thoughts I was having at the time were painful and self-deprecating, so this was liberating. Mindfulness of my thoughts led me to discover, however, that life is more than what my mind was telling me. Mindfulness of our thoughts and emotions simply means becoming aware of them, without judgement and with acceptance.

Our minds also include the experience of our rich diversity of human emotions. We have the capacity to experience such a wonderful array of different feelings. Take some time to notice what emotions you are feeling, too. Similarly to thoughts, they also come and go.

An image I find helpful to illustrate the practice of mindfulness of our thoughts and feelings is to imagine swimming in an ocean. The waves are your thoughts and emotions and they will take you where they please. Now imagine you are on a surfboard, riding the waves and enjoying the ride as the waves come and go. You can even watch the waves go by.

Mindfulness is your surfboard. Your thoughts and emotions are all transitory. If we notice this, they no longer need to dictate our behaviour. For example, if you are having the

thought 'Other people don't like me' and believe it to be true, then you may avoid going out. If you simply acknowledge the thought and how it is not particularly helpful in terms of taking any positive action, you can let it go and make sure you socialize. Of course, riding a surfboard takes a lot of practice, and so does mindfulness. We all fall off the surfboard occasionally. But that's fine. We can just hop right back on. Getting to know your mind is a constant journey to which there is no end; but our experience of the mind is real and part of our lives, so it is a journey worth embarking on.

MINDFULNESS PRACTICE

THE STORIES OF THE THINKING MIND

Our thoughts often take us away from the direct experience of our lives in the present moment. We often get lost and involved in them. But we don't need to. Notice your thoughts in your everyday life. Notice what they are telling you and whether it is true or helpful. You may be surprised to see how many thoughts you have and find it difficult to separate them out. That's OK. Being mindful of your thoughts will get easier with practice. When you notice your thoughts, don't hold on to them or push them away. They all come and go and are constantly changing. Just let them be as they are.

The Habits of the Mind: Origins in a Natural World

As we become more familiar with our minds, we begin to notice that they follow a number of recurring patterns. The thinking mind is brilliant at analysing, planning, categorizing, remembering, communicating, judging and assessing. It is also believed that the majority of thoughts we experience contain negative messages. And although our minds can seem like incessant little dictators challenging our self-esteem, putting us under pressure and causing us to worry about everything, this is completely normal.

Why does the mind do this? Once again, the answer is found in the natural world. Indeed, the mind was created as a problem solver. It evolved to help us solve problems, which would ensure our survival in a natural and social environment. Its main purposes were to avoid life-threatening danger, understand social interactions, communicate with others and ensure we had sufficient access to and control of potential sexual partners, food and territories. The sorts of thoughts that probably went through the minds of our ancestors were messages resulting from their experiences in a dangerous natural world. 'Run away from that bear. Be kind to them, as they have food. Be careful, you never know what might be hiding behind that rock. Make sure you have enough food resources to get you through the winter.' They were messages that ensured our survival, leading to direct action that ensured we would live longer and have more children.

Our minds also enabled us to innovate, create and modify our environments to satisfy our ever-increasing needs and desires. Indeed, ours is the only species present on every continent on the planet, except Antarctica. In the context of its evolution in a natural world hundreds of thousands of years ago, the mind contributed to the overwhelming success of our species in colonizing most of the planet.

Our Minds in a Modern World

When we first evolved, our main purpose was survival and reproduction. Nowadays, fitting into a social group, hoarding food, protecting our territory and avoiding danger are no longer a matter of life or death. In fact, for most of us, they are not even challenges at all.

As survival became less of a concern, our minds began to bring forth another world – a world with language, culture, religion, ideals, beliefs, concepts and ideas of right and wrong. Have you ever thought about where these all come from? They are all products of the mind itself. Before the evolution of our species, none of them existed.

Some creations of the human mind have been wonderful. However, some of the ideals created by our minds have generated a lot of suffering. If you think about it, there is no other animal on Earth that kills its own species in the name of abstract concepts, religion, beliefs and ideals, is there?

The Search for Happiness

In our everyday lives, our minds continue to do the job they evolved for. They are constantly looking out for potential threats and dangers. However, most of the hypothetical dangerous situations that it imagines these days never happen and are rarely life-threatening. In our modern lives, our main purpose has become to achieve so-called 'happiness'. Consequently, we have created a number of stories and images about what 'happiness' might be, and what might lead us to it. We have tried to find meaning in a world where survival is no longer our primary pursuit. This is a natural thing to do, of course. But how have we done it? We have used our minds.

Our minds were built to find solutions to problems and have turned happiness into a problem that we need to solve. What's more, we have imagined the idea that happiness means 'to feel good all the time'. Consequently, we have created a number of potential ideals we should aspire to, which we think will give us a constant state of feeling good, such as having more money, owning a house, having a successful career, being more confident or having a perfect body. These will supposedly all make us 'happier'. What's more, if we do not achieve these ideals, our minds will tell us that 'everybody should be happy', leaving us with a sense of failure to achieve this so-called 'happiness'. Our lives are thus so complicated and diverse that we have become separated from our direct experience and instead are slaves to our minds. We are no longer aware of how our bodies are, what are emotions are, what we are thinking and what is around us. Instead, we choose to distract ourselves from our experience of life all the time in search of constant pleasure. In the context of our modern world, this is the sort of scenario that leads to depression, anxiety, self- doubt and general unhappiness.

WHO ARE WE REALLY?

◆

Our bodies are our natural home — but it seems we have lost the ability to simply be in our bodies. And after all, aren't we 'human beings'? We evolved with the simple purpose of being alive, didn't we? What if simply 'being' as we are right now, enjoying the ride of life, is where 'happiness' lies?

LIVING IN THE REALMS OF OUR MINDS in search of the ultimate answer to becoming happier may be where we are continuing to set ourselves up for seeking something that we will never find. Recent discoveries about what the mind actually is are beginning to confirm this. In the past ten to twenty years, some groundbreaking developments in the world of Western science have led to a slightly different understanding of the mind or self from that usually encountered historically. It seems possible that the existence of a permanent separate fixed mind or 'self', to be found in one single place within us, could be an illusion we have created.

There is growing evidence that the mind and the body may in fact not be two separate entities, after all. Instead, they could be intimately connected. Have you ever noticed how you feel your thoughts and emotions in your body? We tend to feel anxiety in our stomachs, stress as tension in our shoulders, sadness as a lump in our throats, excitement as a racing heartbeat, and anger in our clenched fists. If we have negative thoughts going through our minds, we tend to simultaneously feel increased tension in our bodies. If we have appreciative, positive thoughts going through our minds, however, we tend

MINDFULNESS PRACTICE

FEELING YOUR EMOTIONS

Whether we are happy, sad, hurt or excited, our emotions are at the heart of our experiences every day and our lives would be very boring without them. See if you can become more familiar with your emotions. Notice the bodily sensations that accompany them, notice where you feel them and how intensely you feel them, and let them be as they are. Don't try to eliminate them or hold on to them. They may feel pleasurable, painful or neutral but they are all normal. Simply accept them without judgment and investigate them with gentle curiosity. Our emotions bring us to life.

to feel physically more relaxed. Our thoughts, emotions and general states of mind are intricately linked to the experience we have of our bodies.

A New Understanding

Neuroscientists, biologists, psychologists and cognitive scientists such as Francisco Varela, Humberto Maturana and others are increasingly revealing that there seems to be no such thing as a constant, independent 'self' within each of us that defines our true and fixed identity. If so, then who are we?

This new understanding of what our minds are suggests that our states of mind – our thoughts, feelings, moods, behaviours – are ever-changing. These transitory, continually changing states depend not only on the internal state of our entire bodies, but also on what is going on around us. This means that the unfathomable interplay of these internal and external conditions gives rise to our experience at a given moment. Our conscious awareness of this experience in time is what we tend to call 'mind', 'self' or 'I'. However, although this 'self' has a tendency to follow a number of similar patterns through the development of behavioural habits we all have, it is much more of a process than a fixed tangible entity. Indeed, despite the behavioural habits we tend to form as we live our lives, we can always grow, develop and change as we interact with the world around us, as we come into contact with new people and new experiences.

What Is Your 'I' Telling You Today?

Stop for a moment and consider this. Is the 'I' that we perceive as being ourselves always there? No, it isn't. It comes in and out of our awareness throughout the day. If you are fully engaged in an assignment at work, absorbed in a film, listening to your best friend confiding in you, lost in the beauty of a piece of music, are you aware of this 'I' then? Can you hear it in your mind? Probably not. It also disappears when we fall asleep; it is not the same as when we were children and it is even slightly different today from what it was yesterday. One day it can be telling you that you are looking wonderful, that you are a great success, that it's a beautiful day and that all is right with the world. This may be a day when you have had a long restful night's sleep, a

> *Is the 'I' that we perceive as being ourselves always there?*

delicious hearty breakfast, you received a compliment from a friend and you achieved your daily goal at work. The next day it may tell you that you are failing, that you are no good at your job and that you need to work on becoming a better person. This could be a day where your body is feeling tired and over-worked, it is raining and cold outside, someone criticized you at work or you had an argument with your partner. The point is, our experience of the present moment – our state of mind, our thoughts, our emotions and our resulting overall sense of 'self' or 'mind' – is dependent on an infinite number of conditions, and it is changing all the time.

Catching Up with Buddha

There is an aspect to this scientific conclusion, which many cognitive scientists have arrived at, that is truly fascinating. Indeed, it seems that after years of research and scientific modelling, cognitive science is beginning to come to the same conclusion as the Buddha did 2,500 years ago. When he first experienced Enlightenment, the Buddha sat with a calm, relaxed and open mind. Enlightenment is nothing to do with understanding through knowledge, concepts or intellect. Instead, it is a simple awakening to the nature of life as it is. During his meditation under the Bodhi Tree, the Buddha saw that everything, from the tiniest speck of dust to the rest of the universe, is linked together in a constantly changing pattern. Everything is related and everything that happens has an effect on everything else. As part of this moment of insight, the Buddha also saw into the nature of the mind or self. He taught that our 'self' is not a separate, individual, constant entity. The experience we have of our self is better considered as a by-product of our sensations, our feelings, emotions, thoughts, and awareness of our internal and external worlds at a given moment. It is not what we *think* we are. It is simply what we are in the present moment, and it is ever-changing.

To live in the realms of our minds and to cling to the idea of a constant separate 'I' experiencing our entire lives lies at the heart of most of our unhappiness. This is not surprising. Our experience tells us that we are evolving and that, in reality, there is no permanent separate 'me'. If we hang on to something that isn't there, it is bound to be very frustrating for us all.

As we develop greater awareness of our thoughts, emotions and experience, we begin to gain insight into the fact that life is made of our continuously changing experience. As we learn to accept this and pay more attention to the here and now, we will begin to invite greater freedom and happiness into our lives.

HOW DID WE LOSE TOUCH WITH OUR NATURAL HOME?

Although we come from the natural world and are an integral part of it, are we aware of nature in our everyday lives? Now that we have an insight into the nature of our minds and how they can take us away from our direct experience of our own lives, let's see how they have also separated us from the natural world.

IN ORDER TO UNDERSTAND THIS, we need to think back in time again to when our ancestors were roaming the African savannah. As our minds continued to evolve, so did language, probably between 100,000 and 30,000 years ago. Most people think that language enabled our ancestors to work together more effectively and communicate with other members of their tribes. Being able to talk meant being able to tell each other about where the best hunting grounds were, where to find the most nutritious food supplies, where to avoid poisonous plants, where the dangerous animals were hiding. It was much better for the survival of all members of a tribe if only one person had to encounter a poisonous plant, rather than each member finding out by himself.

As language enabled us to have more sophisticated relationships with others, and as we continued to develop the ability for abstract thought to plan, innovate, imagine and create, we began to pay less attention to nature. Indeed, as we became better and better at protecting ourselves from danger, through better shelters, more secure long-term food supplies, better hunting techniques, it is likely that we didn't really need to be so aware of nature anyway.

When Did It Happen?

It is very difficult to know exactly when we began to lose our connection with the natural world, but the rise of agriculture around 10,000 years ago is thought to have been an important turning point. When we first evolved, we lived nomadic lives, surviving by hunting and gathering food, in tune with the rhythms of the natural world. When there were abundant sources of wild game, fruit and vegetables, we would thrive. When food was scarce or weather conditions unfavourable, we would simply endure the times of scarcity. We took what nature offered us at the time and we only took enough to satisfy our basic needs. When our minds gave rise to the practice of agriculture, we began to cultivate single crops and move towards a sedentary lifestyle. This led to the emergence of villages, towns and cities. We began to domesticate wild grains and animals and were able to store surplus food. We started to modify our natural environment, irrigate our crops, select which plants and animals we wanted to keep alive and kill those we didn't want around. Our food was actively grown and became a commodity that we could sell as we started to produce more than we needed for subsistence.

As towns and cities began to grow, denser populations began to form and larger societies gave rise to the development of the political and economic systems we use to organize our lives. Most of these had very little connection with the natural world. In fact, they were at odds with it. Indeed, as we moved towards a greater sense of power and control over the world around us, our political and economic systems were focused on the exploitation of nature as an infinite resource at the service of our endless needs and desires. Ever since then,

---

We are disconnected from nature, we are wounded
from the Spirit outward, and that has caused the largest
majority of the problems that plague the world today.

FROM 'THE CIRCLE WITHIN', DIANNE SYLVAN
LLEWELLYN WORLDWIDE, WOODBURY, USA, 2003

and at an ever-increasing speed, we have continued to supplement our lives with the development of efficient technology, increasing levels of comfort, control and security. For most of us in our modern lives, we now have comfortable warm houses, easy access to endless supplies of food, televisions, mobile phones and the Internet.

It is rather frightening how quickly we have moved away from our natural home, from the hunter-gatherer way of life whereby we belonged to nature, to a way of life that enacts a very different story: 'Nature belongs to us'. Who invented this story? Our minds once again. Notice how well we are enacting it. Yet it is nature that has provided us with a body, food, shelter and a mind, in order for us to get to where we are now. Nature gave us life and sustains our life. This is a fact we seem to have forgotten, with serious consequences for all life on our planet.

Losing Awareness of Nature

Today, our minds and lifestyles keep us separate from the natural world more than ever. The contents of our minds revolve around worries, memories, ideals, beliefs, judgemental stories and fixed ideas of what might make us happy. Of course, for immediate survival purposes, bringing our awareness to the natural world is not required in our modern comfortable lives. However, this means that instead we have the luxury of being able to simply experience the joy of being a part of nature, the simple pleasure of feeling part of life itself. And given our origins and the fact that we *are* nature, this could be the most natural and fulfilling experience in the world.

So many of us rarely take time to appreciate the beauty of the sunlight through new leaves on the trees or the peace there is in feeling a gentle breeze against our faces. We don't take time to notice the beautiful iridescent head of a mallard in the park or the blue sheen on the wings of a magpie in the garden. Instead, we are too busy wrapped up in our busy lives, rushing around as fast as we can to be as efficient and productive as possible. As our minds dictate our lives, we prefer to focus on stress, or distract ourselves texting our friends, or block out the outside world completely by listening to our music all the time. We leave little space for appreciation and contemplation of the simple things around us when the opportunity to marvel at the natural world is everywhere, at every moment. It is in us and around us and it provides us with most of the things we have in our lives.

As we are not aware of it, we spend less time actively experiencing it. A recent study by the Nature Conservancy showed that getting outside to experience the natural world just doesn't come naturally to us any more. When asked what they'd do with a day to themselves, for example, twice as many people would meet up with friends for a meal as would meet them for an outdoors walk. And if they aren't spending time with their friends, people are more likely to spend a day

off lying in front of the television or going to the cinema. Of course, there is nothing wrong with enjoying the warmth and cosiness of our homes or a trip to the cinema, but 10 per cent of us don't spend any time in nature at all.

We have also forgotten that we depend on nature for our food, clothing, houses and medicines. Many of us don't really think of food at any stage before it reaches the supermarket. We forget that most of our clothing comes from plants such as cotton. We are no longer aware that in order to get rid of our headaches, we use aspirin made from willow-bark extract.

The 'Nature' Label

Our minds like to organize the world into separate little boxes. It makes them feel more in control and consequently less threatened. The word 'nature' is commonly used to describe the rest of the natural world, without people – but if you stop and think about it, it is simply a label we have given, separating two things from each other. It is another product of the mind; before the evolution of the mind and language, names and categories did not exist. Creating artificial separation between humans and nature, the same way we created a separation between our 'self' and our bodies, is denying the reality of life once again. Living our lives based on the idea that we are all separate from each other and from our natural home and all the life within it is at the heart of most of the suffering on our planet.

Beyond Separation & Categories

Our minds have a tendency to divide our experience of life into separate categories in order to help us make sense of it and communicate it. They create fixed labels to classify what we feel, think and see. However, this is not a true reflection of our direct experience. Everything is constantly changing and flowing and everything is interconnected, not isolated.

This applies to our sense of 'self'. We perceive a separate, constant, fixed 'I' experiencing our lives, but this is a creation of the mind. Our 'self' is a pattern of thoughts and behaviours that we can become aware of through mindfulness of our thoughts and emotions. This pattern is constantly changing.

This also applies to the natural world. Everything in the natural world is interlinked. What do we call a tree? Usually we are referring to its trunk, branches and leaves, but this is a label we have created that separates out one part of the tree. Below the ground, its roots extend into the soil and absorb minerals. The tree also obtains carbon dioxide and absorbs water and sunlight. What we call a tree does not exist as a tree in isolation of all the things to which it is connected.

The separation between our 'self', 'other humans' and 'nature' is beginning to have disastrous consequences for life on Earth, as it denies that what we do to nature we do to other humans, and to ourselves.

WHY IS AWARENESS OF THE
NATURAL WORLD IMPORTANT?

◆

Losing awareness of our natural world is having deep consequences for our own well-being, as well as for the well-being of other species we share the planet with. However, our own well-being is interlinked with that of the rest of life on Earth. There is no separation between us. So what is happening to nature is also happening to us.

To LOSE AWARENESS OF THE NATURAL WORLD is to deny an inherent and vital part of being alive and human. We have replaced our natural home with comfortable and secure lifestyles. Many of us spend much of our time in cities, in front of televisions and computers, on our phones and communicating electronically. When we began to seek protection from the life-threatening dangers of the natural world, we were trying to avoid death. Now, however, by locking ourselves up indoors and in our minds, it seems we are beginning to avoid life. Technology and more comfortable lives are part of our world and we can't deny this. And personally, I do not intend to return to a hunter-gatherer lifestyle. However, we also need to maintain the experience of nature in our lives.

This disconnection with the natural world has led to what Richard Louv called 'Nature Deficit Disorder', whereby many of us – and especially our children – are suffering from anxiety, depression, hyperactivity, attention deficit disorders, obesity and diabetes. There is evidence also that excessive stimulation from technological or artificial means can cause mental fatigue and loss of vitality and general health. In a world where living in the realms of our minds can take over to the extent where mental-health problems are a global epidemic, our loss of awareness of the natural world is not something we can continue to ignore. We need the rest of the natural world for our own well-being.

Creating an Unnatural World

Our loss of awareness of the natural world is also at the heart of infinite decline, destruction and suffering for all living beings. By creating the concept of nature being separate from ourselves, we have proceeded to exploit it in order to satisfy our every desire. We are cutting down the world's forests, destroying other natural habitats, polluting the air, land and seas, fishing life out of the oceans, displacing plants and animals across the globe and exhausting natural resources. Meanwhile, human activities are also accelerating the rate of global climate change, which could lead to more loss of plants and animals, more frequent natural disasters, disease, sea-level rise and acidification of the oceans. These are all leading to the extinction of animals and plants at an unprecedented rate since the dinosaurs disappeared sixty million years ago.

Are these consequences surprising? Not really. The processes that sustain life in the natural world follow some basic laws and our controlling minds have convinced us that we may be able to override them. If we continue to believe this, and live by the story 'nature belongs to us', we are likely to cause the collapse of all life on Earth as we know it. We won't be exempt from this, because we don't exist without the rest of the natural world. The products of the human mind, our abstract ideals, our beliefs, our political systems, our economic systems will never persist if they continue to assume that we are separate from nature. Think about the natural law of gravity. We all have direct experience of this. Would you ever try to defy gravity? Would you ever go and jump off a cliff and hope to stay alive? Almost certainly not.

It is the same with the other rules that govern the natural world. When we bring our awareness to nature, we soon understand that one of the essential natural laws is interconnectedness. Life is fundamentally one. We *are* life. What we do to one part of life, we do to the rest of life, including ourselves. The eventual consequence of denying that nature is sustaining our life on this planet could be the end of humanity itself. The Buddha saw this from beneath the Bodhi Tree. Ecologists see this from their scientific research. However we look at it, this is an undeniable reality. Reconnecting with nature through mindfulness is consequently vital if we are to reverse this extremely concerning trend. Bringing our awareness back to nature lies at the heart of our happiness and of the well-being of all life on Earth.

CHAPTER THREE

COMING
BACK TO LIFE

*Coming back to life here and now is at the
heart of enhancing the well-being of all life on
Earth, including our own. Living in the realms of
our minds has removed us from the simple joy of being
alive. It has caused a lot of suffering for ourselves
and for all other living things. But nature is part of us,
we need it. Notice, experience and enjoy a little bit
of nature every day. Bring your awareness back to
our amazing, mysterious, unfathomable and
wondrous natural world.*

NATURAL PEACE OF MIND

◆

The naturalist and explorer Charles Waterton was one of the first people in the Western world to show an understanding of the importance of nature and its protection for our well-being. At a time when the industrial revolution was driving the proliferation of coal mines and factories, resulting in the pollution and destruction of the countryside, he decided to take action to protect the land he owned.

CHARLES WATERTON was a wealthy aristocratic landowner who lived in the early 1800s and was truly passionate about the natural world. Sir David Attenborough claims that Waterton was 'one of the first people anywhere to recognize, not only that the natural world was of great importance, but that it needed protection as humanity made more and more demands on it'.

Waterton was a pioneer, creating the first ever proper nature reserve – a bird sanctuary for the protection of wildfowl, a group that included geese, ducks and swans. In order to isolate it from increasing industrialization, he built a tall wall around his estate. He then invited guests to come and visit his estate and enjoy spending time watching the birds through his telescopes. He is said to have encouraged patients with psychological disorders from the local psychiatric institution to come and spend time simply sitting and watching the birds. He claimed that it gave them peace of mind.

By bringing our awareness to the rest of the natural world, we can all invite greater calm, serenity and simplicity into our lives. We all feel stressed, anxious or upset on occasions. These feelings are very common in the busy lives we lead today, but in times like these, the rest of nature can be a best friend to us all. We just need to invite it into our lives.

An Alternative Quick Fix

When we experience painful thoughts and emotions, what do we usually do? We seek something that will fix them quickly. We may force ourselves to ignore them, distract ourselves by watching television or reach for that tempting bar of chocolate. Our tendency is to find strategies for getting rid of these thoughts and feelings in the quickest and easiest way. We try to push them away and replace them with instant feelings of pleasure. Why wouldn't we? No one wants to feel pain. It is a perfectly natural reaction to try to avoid it. The thing is, we soon notice that trying to rid ourselves of negative feelings often increases our suffering. We start fighting a losing battle.

It is best to accept our feelings as they are, without letting them take over our lives. We can hop on our surfboard of awareness and ride the waves. Next time you feel stressed, anxious or hurt, try this approach instead. Bring your attention to your thoughts – they might be thoughts such as 'I have so much to do', 'I'll never manage this job in time' or 'I'm useless' – and just notice them without judging. We all have them in our lives and we always will. Become aware of any tension or other sensations in your body and let them be also. Then stop for a moment, walk outside and find a little bit of nature to be with. It doesn't need to be for very long. It could just be for ten minutes. Take yourself somewhere there are trees, birds, flowers, fresh air, maybe a river or a pond. Bring your attention to what you can see, feel, hear and smell and just notice everything around you. Allow yourself to simply enjoy that moment. Then return to your task.

Walk It Off...

Walking in nature helps me clear my mind and reflect upon the challenges of everyday life with greater clarity. The natural world is my number-one remedy when I feel stressed. Sometimes, if I have had an argument with someone or I'm worried about a particular problem at work, my mind gets obsessively caught up in analysing the situation over and over again. By engaging with these thoughts, I rarely come to a positive and practical solution. Instead, I get increasingly stressed about the problem and fail to take any action at all. I find that taking a walk out in a forest, across fields or by the sea often helps my mind to come up with the best course of action to take. Walking in wide open spaces in particular gives me a great sense of freedom and makes me feel that time is no longer significant. It gives my thinking mind a rest and helps me review the problem with a new perspective.

...Or Simply Sit with It

Peace is also to be found in simply sitting with nature. Often when we are walking outdoors, we have a destination, even if it is simply the satisfaction of completing the walk. We need to keep moving, to have a purpose. Very rarely do we take the time just to sit down and enjoy the simple pleasure of being. Quietly sitting, with awareness, gives our minds the chance to be calm. It offers the opportunity to experience the beauty and simplicity of stillness. It shows our minds that it's OK to stop. By giving yourself a few minutes to do this, you may discover things you had never been aware of before.

I often seek out tranquil places to simply sit and open up my awareness to the life around me. I begin to enjoy simple pleasures, such as watching the branches of the trees gently giving in to the flow of a breeze without a hint of resistance. Sometimes, the rustling of leaves reminds me of the sound of a distant waterfall. I enjoy noticing where the light touches all the different life forms around me and how it changes the look of the world. I luxuriate in a sense of childish naivety as I watch the clouds in the sky, letting their different shapes and textures capture my imagination. I look out for any birds, noticing how their flight differs between species. Many seabirds glide over the ocean, crows and pigeons have a more frequent wing beat, woodpeckers have an undulating flight and swallows swoop and weave their way in pursuit of insects. I take a closer look at the plants and animals close to me, such

Still Waters

I find still waters infinitely soothing. Sometimes, the water is so still that the reflection is perfect; but I love how a quiet breeze creates gentle ripples and how the ripples distort the reflection of the world above. When I watch for long enough, I feel infused with a sense of gentle calm. An internal quietening comes over me as my mind relaxes and I feel as if the placidity of the water becomes part of me.

as the beautiful patterns and colours on the petals of a flower, the texture and scents of different leaves and grasses, the curious fungal growths and lichens on the bark of a tree and the intricate bodies of insects in the grass. I marvel at the fact that everything is constantly changing, and the soft thrum of life around me fascinates my senses and calms my agitated mind.

Infinite Serenity

Some places I have visited have gifted me with a glimpse of universal stillness where the chattering mind has no place at all. These are places where all my senses are brought to attention in a moment. I have experienced the absolute silence that engulfs everything after a night of heavy snow falling across a landscape of rolling countryside. I have been filled with the tranquillity of magnificent lakes surrounded by mountains,

where all I could hear were the echoes of the silence of the mountains and the soft lapping of the water against the rocks. I have sat on the summit of mountains and contemplated views of boundless rainforests extending beyond the horizon, where not a single sound can be heard, despite the fact that, inside, the forests are teeming with life. These unforgettable moments have left me with a sense of infinite serenity.

Stress? Who Needs It

We know that spending time in the company of our natural world reduces stress levels, quietens the mind and improves concentration and focus. Going for a walk, sitting on a bench in the park, spending time by the sea are all known to relieve stress and improve concentration and creativity. Natural views have stress-reducing effects on people at work, in prisons, in hospitals and even when driving. Spending time outdoors has been shown to reduce nervous-system activity

◆

Climb the mountains and get their good tidings.
Nature's peace will flow into you as sunshine flows
into trees. The winds will blow their own freshness into
you, and the storms their energy, while cares
will drop off like autumn leaves.

JOHN MUIR (1838–1914)
AMERICAN NATURALIST & WRITER

◆

and levels of the stress hormone cortisol in our bodies. A still, aware and less distracted mind means a greater ability to be present and concentrated in our daily activities.

In our modern lives we are constantly rushing around trying to achieve our never-ending to-do lists. Our minds convince us that there is no time to stop. In urban environments our minds are constantly stimulated at an unnatural rate. They are not adapted to that level and rate of input. They evolved to process and affiliate with the natural world, not the increasingly fast-paced hustle and bustle of our cities. After a day in a big city full of people, traffic, advertising, loud noises and the constant rush and fast pace of life, my mind feels scattered and exhausted. Nature gives the thinking mind a rest, opens up our senses and collects thoughts into a gentle focus.

Getting out into the wild itself is obviously the best experience you will have of the natural world. However, we can begin our mindfulness of the natural world through simpler steps in our everyday lives. We can carry a card depicting a beautiful natural place with us to look at and appreciate occasionally throughout the day. We could set the screensaver on our computer to an image of our favourite animal, plant or wild place. We can listen to recordings of natural sounds or bring some of our favourite natural places to mind. There are endless ways in which we can bring nature and the calm it offers us into our everyday lives. Treasure it. There are not many sources of true calm in the lives we lead.

THE TONIC OF WILDNESS

◆

Nature is our life. It contains pure vital energy we can all connect with. The American author and naturalist Henry David Thoreau wrote, 'We need the tonic of wildness.' To him, living without nature meant depriving ourselves of the experience of the deepest truth of life. How can we do that to ourselves?

ALREADY, BACK IN THE NINETEENTH CENTURY, Thoreau was concerned that we were dulling our senses, our experience of life and our minds by removing ourselves from nature and living our lives in fixed habitual ruts, distracting ourselves only with unfulfilling entertainment. Instead, the natural world brought his sensory body to life and enabled him to think with freedom and creativity.

Even just spending twenty minutes a day outdoors can increase vitality and boost our physical and mental energy. If I spend too long indoors, inactive or engaging in activities where I am only using my thinking mind, I begin to feel sluggish, tired and mentally fatigued. When feeling like this, heading out into the wild is often the last thing we feel like doing. Instead we'd rather curl up in bed or drink coffee to wake ourselves up. It is actually now proven that getting into nature is a better solution with better results. Try going outside for a brisk walk, cycle or a run instead. Enjoy being active and soak up all that nature has to offer along the way.

◆

Sunshine is delicious, rain is refreshing, wind braces
us up, snow is exhilarating, there is really no such thing
as bad weather, only different kinds of good weather.

JOHN RUSKIN (1819–1900)
ART CRITIC & PHILANTHROPIST

◆

When it comes to boosting our energy levels, cold, rainy, wild weather is sometimes particularly effective. I recently cycled home from the office in torrential rain. When the rain started, my first reaction was to think: 'Oh no…not now!' I noticed my mind interpreting the event negatively and decided to let that thought go and embrace the experience instead. I knew it didn't matter if I got wet, I could simply change my clothes when I got home. So instead, I just enjoyed the sensory experience and it became an exhilarating ride. The rain refreshed me and, as the drops trickled down my face and dripped out of my hair, I felt as if I had been naturally cleansed and invigorated after a long day in the office.

Being Alive

The vitality of the natural world can be very powerful. Nature's expression of life and all its diversity can make us feel truly alive. I remember once sitting at the top of a cliff, overlooking the ocean. The midday sunshine warmed my face with its radiance. The contrasting colours of the flowers and

grass, the lichens on the rocks and the sea below were intensely vibrant. As I looked down, I could see enormous waves rising, then crashing against large boulders. They propelled impressive clouds of spray towards the sky and onto my skin. There were four gulls gliding above me, maintaining their balance in the wind and casting their shadows on the ground next to me. Over the rocky beach beneath me, two swallows were swooping back and forth with amazing agility and speed. The exuberant scent of the salt-infused damp air mixed with the sweet smell from the flowers was delicious and uplifting. It was wonderful to feel so alive.

Water can be a source of both calm and energy. Any time I am close to mountains and rivers, I will seek out waterfalls, one of my favourite features of the natural world. I can sit and enjoy cascading waterfalls for hours. The overwhelming roar of the white waters, the cold spray, the pure freshness they create in the air around them and the lush green vegetation that often grows beside them are intensely invigorating. They fill me with a sense of purity, life and freedom. I remember once when travelling in the tropics spending a few hours at a waterfall in a rainforest. I sat on the damp rocks by the plunge pool, absorbing the majesty of the sight. It was one of the highest waterfalls I have ever seen. Bathing in the plunge pool, floating on my back and looking up at the water crashing down from high above me was an awesome moment. I felt as if I had connected with life at its very source.

Embodying Life

Henry David Thoreau is famous for having undertaken a two-year experiment when he went to live a simple life in the woods in a self-built house near Walden Pond in Massachusetts, USA. This is where he wrote his book *Walden: or, Life in the Woods*. While there, he learnt from nature through the experience of all his senses and he witnessed the natural world's ever-changing creations unfolding around him, within him and through him in perpetual flow. He came to see the body as a natural temple for us all, an opportunity to embody life, through the awareness of all our natural senses.

In our Western world, we tend to put our thinking minds before our bodies. We live in the world of our thoughts and forget the gift of life we have within our bodies. Our bodies are our fleeting expression of life in this universe. Being alienated from our direct experience of them, as we spend more time working at computers, worrying, planning and analysing, can lead us to become disconnected from life itself and

---

I went to the woods because I wished to live
deliberately, to front only the essential facts of life, and
see if I could not learn what it had to teach, and not,
when I came to die, discover that I had not lived.

HENRY DAVID THOREAU (1817–62)
AMERICAN WRITER, PHILOSOPHER & NATURALIST

MINDFULNESS PRACTICE

THE BODY SCAN

✳

To live in our bodies is vital. They are our opportunity to incarnate life. The body scan is a great practice to help us let go of the contents of our minds and get back in touch with our bodies. During the practice, try to cultivate a gentle curiosity about your experience. Become interested in your body and any sensations you may find there. Lie down comfortably on your back. Become aware of how your body feels against the floor. Take a few slow, deep breaths and pay attention to the resulting sensations. Feel how and where your body moves as you breathe. Then bring your attention down to your feet. What do they feel like? Are they cold or warm? Are they relaxed or tense? If you feel nothing in particular, that is fine too. Bring all other parts of your body into your awareness one by one in a similar fashion and notice any sensations. Are they pleasurable, painful or neutral? Do they change or stay the same? Can you feel any tension in any parts of your body? Whatever sensations you find, don't try to change them, or judge them. Just let them be. As thoughts appear in your mind, just notice these, and gently come back to the sensations of your breath and in your body. Enjoy exploring how your body feels and how your experience of it changes constantly.

MINDFULNESS PRACTICE

SWEET SCENTS OF NATURE

✳

Becoming aware of our natural senses is the best way to reconnect with nature. Natural scents are present everywhere, if we pay attention to them. For instance, you may notice the scent of freshly cut grass in a city park, the exotic citrus scent of orange blossom or the musty scent of fungi in woodland. One of my favourite places to enjoy mindfulness of natural scents is a herb garden. Your local botanic gardens may have one – or you could grow your own. Herbs are rich in a range of essential oils that have powerful fragrances. Try gently brushing your hand against one of the herbs. Then close your eyes and familiarize yourself with its scent. Is it sweet, aromatic or spicy? Does it remind you of anything? Is it pleasant? Do this with different herbs. You could also try crushing a leaf between your fingers for even more intense aromas. Simply explore the wonderful variety of nature's scents. Many plants have distinctive smells – become aware of them and investigate wherever you are. You don't even need to know what the plants are. This exercise requires no knowledge whatsoever. Just enjoy the sweet scents of nature.

dampen our experience of being alive. Living from the body is vital. Our bodies are at home in nature – this is where they belong. We can bring awareness to our bodies by practising a daily 'body scan'. Notice how your body feels, enjoy discovering how your experience of your body changes, and notice what new sensations you might find in different parts of it.

Engage Your Senses

Our senses are our direct connection with the world around us. They allow us to invite life into our being. Take joy in your senses. Experiment with them. They are a very precious part of us. I love the intoxicating scents of wild flowers on a warm summer's day, the freshness of the air in a forest after it has rained, the resinous fragrance of pine forests as they heat up in the sun and the soft sponginess of moss growing on rocks. I like experiencing a mix of childish fear and excitement when I see a flash of lightning and hear the dramatic sound of thunder during a storm. The red and black polka-dot pattern of a ladybird against the vibrant green of a leaf, the striking colours of flower petals against their foliage and the bright orange of a blackbird's beak against its black plumage never fail to uplift me. And who doesn't feel a sense of wonder when observing the changing colours in the sky as the sun rises and sets? Smell, watch, touch, taste, listen to nature as often as you can. We can all discover how much life we hold in us that way.

Exercising in Nature

The energizing effect of exercising out in nature is a great source of vitality for us all. We now know that the 'feel-good' effect of exercising outdoors goes beyond the purely physical health benefits, to increased vitality, positivity, energy and psychological well-being. Being outdoors enhances our experience of exercise due to our innate connection with all living things. Gradually we tend to enjoy it more and consequently we are more likely to stick to regularly being active.

If we go to our local gym, we can all get our natural endorphins pumping round our bodies on an exercise bike or running machine. This will make us feel good; it may support us to maintain a healthy weight and keep our bodies fit. The gym is a controlled experience and sometimes it is the most convenient way for us to exercise. Going to the gym also means you won't get wet and cold in the rain, or dirty in the mud, or need to face the variability of nature trails. It is usually a predictable experience. However, from time to time, try experiencing the thrill of exercising in the company of nature.

A Nocturnal Ride

I have a friend who is passionate about mountain biking. He told me that nature brought unanticipated movement and beauty to his ride. When riding through wooded single tracks, he really pays attention to the trail; he can smell it and learn about the soil by the way his tyres squidge and slide around

corners. He notices every root and any slight bank in a corner that becomes a possibility to gain momentum. No trail is ever the same; it is a whole new adventure every time.

He once shared with me a particular experience of the first time he rode at night. With handlebar-mounted lights, he couldn't look around corners until he was already upon them and his movements felt almost robotic. Being scratched on the shoulders by frosted holly spikes felt to him as if the forest was scraping away at his comfort zone. Every undulation was a playground. Unexpectedly during his ride, a white form appeared directly above him: a barn owl, drifting through the trees. He was riding through moonlit woodland full of life and wonder. With a smile, his shoulders loosened and the balls of his feet engaged with the pedals. As the owl banked and arced silently around a tree, he felt his body weight flow with the bike. He said: 'There's a moment when it all clicks into place. You don't notice it happen but afterwards you realize that you have no concept of how much time has passed. You become part of the trail as much as the bike is an extension of your body.'

Exercising in nature can capture your attention so much more than when exercising indoors. The unpredictability of the experience naturally leads us to greater awareness of our movements as they become more and more in tune with everything surrounding us, inviting a mysterious and uplifting sense of harmony into our experience.

Natural Creativity

◆

As well as energizing our bodies, the natural world can invigorate our minds. Undoubtedly, an energized, grounded, healthy and active body gives rise to an alive, creative, happier and healthier mind. Abandoning ourselves to the flow of our creative side is our greatest potential to express, share and embody life. It is what makes our minds such astonishing wonders of the natural world.

WE ALL HAVE CREATIVE POTENTIAL. Beyond narrating negative stories to us, our minds are also a wonderful source of imagination and innovation. Our creativity is a very important part of us – it enables us to express ourselves and reflect upon the experiences we have in our lives. Creativity is largely the ability to bring forth original, imaginative products through innovative thinking or artistic expression.

Spending time in nature has been shown to boost our creativity. The reason behind this seems to be that in our everyday lives our attention is constantly occupied by our phones, our computers, our televisions, the general business of our lives, and so on. This causes constant activation of what we call our 'executive attention'. As our attention is drawn from one thing to another, we begin to deplete our ability to engage in more creative, fun and playful thinking. It seems that spending time with nature can refresh our minds by allowing us to expand our attention beyond our consciously thinking mind

and letting the mind wander. At times, it comes up with new and exciting ideas or thoughts, often when we least expect it. Who wants to lose their ability to dream and imagine?

Daydreaming

I often find that when I am in wild places, my mind begins to playfully daydream as I connect with the natural world around me. I wonder what it would feel like to fly like a bird across the mountains and oceans. I imagine myself under the sea and try to gain a sense of what it might be like to swim my way through life like a fish. I start to contemplate what it would be like to be an animal or a plant without a conscious mind. I allow myself to drift in and out of asking myself questions I may never be able to answer and simply savour letting go to the inquisitiveness and curiosity of my childlike imagination.

Being with nature also leads my thoughts to engage with the things that are truly important to me. I often think about my family, my close friends and my passions, such as nature, music and travel. Mysteriously, my mind begins to free itself a little from the habitual thinking patterns it develops in the context of the routine of my everyday life. As it tunes in to the sights, scents and sounds of the natural world, it embarks on an unpredictable journey full of dreams and fantasies. I start to enjoy engaging with my deepest aspirations and I begin thinking with enthusiasm and inspiration about how I could create change in my life to achieve them.

Every Child Is Born a Naturalist

The tonic of nature is also essential for children as they grow up. It seems we are exacerbating the problem of Nature Deficit Disorder by protecting our children from direct contact with the natural world. Do we really want to protect our children from life itself? Every child has an innate fascination and curiosity about the natural world and we need to encourage their exposure to it at a very young age. It seems children are no longer given the opportunity to spend time out in nature exploring, playing and discovering natural wonders. Instead they spend more time in front of computers and televisions in safe environments that protect them from any possible risks. Most of their time is dedicated to constructive, educational, purposeful activities that are often supervised and interactive. The opportunity to engage in spontaneous exploration of their own experience has become very limited.

Free and unstructured play in nature is vital for the development of the bodies and minds of young children. We need to encourage children to be mindful of the natural world as

---

Every child is born a naturalist. His eyes are,

by nature, open to the glories of the stars, the beauty

of the flowers, and the mystery of life.

ANNE SCOTT-JAMES (1913–2009)
ENGLISH JOURNALIST AND AUTHOR

---

well. They need to explore nature with all their senses, climb trees, interact with wild animals and plants, make up their own games, daydream in their special natural places, look for nature's treasures such as shells and feathers – and, above all, enjoy themselves. Playing in nature where things are constantly changing improves children's coordination, awareness, concentration, creativity, independence and ability to cooperate. Let them play hide-and-seek in the woods, catch creepy-crawlies, build dens and pick blackberries. Let's encourage our children to discover their natural home and live its adventures. They will be happier and healthier for it.

HAPPINESS FOR US ALL

Who doesn't want to be happy? There is compelling evidence that having the natural world in our lives makes us happier. We seem to show increased levels of satisfaction with our job, home and life in general when we have natural settings nearby. Spending time with the natural world also improves our mood, reduces depression and anxiety and increases self-esteem.

THE NATURAL WORLD also seems to encourage us to pursue our aspirations for personal development, close relationships and greater community spirit (which in turn can increase our well-being) and reduces our desire to become richer and own more possessions (which are often associated with feelings of dissatisfaction). As we become happier and more open to the rest of life, we also become more caring and generous towards other people when we connect with nature.

Nature often makes me smile. The sight of a beautiful butterfly, the joyful flight and song of a skylark, the playfulness of young mammals and the excitement I feel when I see a rainbow bring joy to my life. I also love the unpredictability of the natural world – the fact that you never know what you might see or hear. There is always a certain mystery and sense of playfulness and exploration in my experience of it. It fills me with a childish sense of wonder, which is very special. We can all learn to look at the natural world with childish curiosity.

A Shared Moment

I have witnessed and enjoyed many occasions where the natural world has instantly uplifted the spirits of people around me. One of my favourites is when people who have never met each other start to marvel at the natural world and connect over it. They laugh at it, smile at it and share their appreciation of it. I remember sitting outside a café in the sunshine. To my surprise, a song thrush hopped onto my table. People at the other tables around me started discussing how beautiful the bird was, exclaimed how lucky we were to have such a close encounter and what a beautiful song these birds have. Everyone opened up and connected over a simple, yet wondrous natural moment. This also happens when on a walk in

MINDFULNESS PRACTICE

TUNE IN TO BIRDSONG

✱

The best time to listen to birdsong is during the dawn or evening chorus. These are often special peaceful times, free of other distracting sounds. Begin by taking a few deep breaths and become aware of your thoughts and feelings. Let them be as they are. Then close your eyes and begin to tune in to any birds singing around you. Familiarize yourself with each of the different songs. Enjoy this simple pleasure of connecting with one of the most beautiful sounds of the natural world.

the countryside – people you may never have met will comment on what a beautiful day it is. I love these moments. We can all find reasons to wonder and smile at the natural world.

One particular natural phenomenon has been shown to contribute to our happiness: birdsong. It seems that it can increase our well-being in all the ways we have just explored – help us relax, energize us, improve our mood and help us concentrate. It is said that birdsong is reassuring for us, as when birds sing, danger is usually absent. The dawn chorus in particular brings our minds to life, as it signals the beginning of a new day. Next time you are awake early in the morning, take a moment to listen to this mesmerizing symphony of life.

NATURAL MINDFULNESS

◆

The happiness we find in the natural world is irreplaceable and it is something we can all connect with. It is in all of us. Our innate affiliation with the natural world means that when we spend time in nature's company, we can open up to letting contentment, ease, peace and vitality into our lives.

So why does nature make us happier? Well, it is perhaps not surprising as it is where we come from and where we belong, it is our home. However, there is also evidence that nature enhances our capacity for mindfulness and reduces the time we spend engaged in worry and rumination over life's problems. Nature captures our sensory experience, our curiosity and our attention and naturally brings us out of our thinking minds and back to the present moment. So it seems that becoming more mindful of the natural world actually enhances our mindfulness of our experience in other parts of our lives. Nature is thus an excellent companion along the path of developing greater awareness and inviting greater happiness into our everyday lives.

Opening Up to Life

When the natural world truly captivated my senses for the first time in Huerquehue National Park, I tuned back in to life. Following this experience, I began to bring my awareness to the natural world more every day. As I opened up and learnt to connect to the rest of life, I began to bring my awareness back to my true experience of myself. I paid greater attention to my senses and gained greater awareness of my body and of my thoughts and emotions. I also began to feel greater meaning in my life as I discovered that my purpose was simply to be alive and enjoy being part of the web of life.

When I am present in wild places, I feel more able to express my authentic self. I can let go of any inhibitions, labels, doubts and insecurities created by my mind. Nature doesn't put any pressure on me. It doesn't judge me or make any demands of me. The natural world gives me a sense of freedom. It just allows me to be with it, as I am, however I am feeling. When I have time in nature, I feel connected with the rest of life and no longer alone. I think of all other living things as being part of my family and this gives me a sense of comfort and belonging.

To me, one of the most special experiences we can have in our lives is to share a chance encounter with the wild. I have

Now I see the secret of the making of
the best persons. It is to grow in the open air,
and to eat and sleep with the earth.

WALT WHITMAN (1819–92)
AMERICAN POET, ESSAYIST & HUMANIST

watched a pygmy-owl as he stared straight down at me from a branch in a tree in the heart of the rainforest. I have come across wild deer as they silently emerged from behind a tree and gazed towards me with a touch of wild innocence. I have relished the sudden sight of a tiny wren as it furtively hopped out of the understorey for a second before disappearing again. I have come across nightjars at dusk, silently flying over the heathlands. I have stumbled across precious hummingbirds in their exquisite, minuscule nests. When I have shared these encounters with others, they cause the immediate quietening of our speech to a gentle whisper. I have also enjoyed simple moments watching a bumblebee foraging by my side or an inquisitive robin exploring my garden for food. The indecipherable secrecy and elusiveness of these encounters will never cease to fill me with a sense of wonder, humility and respect. These unique occasions of intimacy with the wild make me feel as if I need nothing else in the world but to be there, in that moment. They make me feel privileged to be alive.

Bring your awareness back to the natural world and open up to life.

Bring your awareness back to the natural world and open up to life. We need the rest of nature. Mindfulness of the natural world encourages us to shift our attention away from the questioning, worrying, problem-seeking mind and back to our full experience of our home, here and now. As Thoreau

put it, we can 'open up all our pores and bathe in all the tides of nature'. Put aside time to savour the natural world. Notice it, explore it and savour it. At times it will surprise you. At others it will challenge you. Every now and then it will puzzle you. And when you are least expecting it, the natural world may occasionally secretly gift you with that intimate glimpse of its wondrous mystery.

MINDFULNESS PRACTICE
FIND YOUR SECRET NATURE SPOT

Find a secret place you particularly like or appreciate, close to your home and easy to get to, where you can regularly go and spend time in solitude with nature. Remember that your only purpose when you are there is to soak up the natural world with all your attention. Cultivate an intimate interest in your secret spot. Try to visit a few times a week. Notice how the place changes. See how your experience of it changes. Spending time in your secret nature spot becomes an opportunity for a moment of stillness in your busy life, when you can get to know and explore a little patch of the natural world.

CHAPTER FOUR

MEDITATIONS ON BEAUTY & WISDOM

*As we develop our awareness of the
natural world, we begin to appreciate
the beauty of nature as an end in itself. So
many artists and scientists have been inspired
by their experiences of nature. We too can let
ourselves be infused by the endless beauty and
wisdom of the natural world, and integrate this
into our own lives. Looking deeper into nature
will lead us to participating more fully in the
unfolding of the wonderful diversity of life.*

DEEPENING APPRECIATION

◆

Mindfulness is a skill and, like all skills, it requires practice. When we first go out into nature, we may find it dull, and wish we were at home, doing something seemingly more exciting. We may notice ourselves trying to find pleasure in it but feel nothing and end up disheartened. This is perfectly natural. It takes time to see the beauty there is in simplicity.

B E PATIENT WITH YOURSELF and persevere in bringing yourself back to what is around you. Practice is the key to altering the mind's habits. Notice your mind wishing to be elsewhere. Be aware of it wandering in search of immediate pleasure or focusing on a problem that's bothering you. Then gently bring yourself back to the sights and sounds around you. Just keep remembering that word 'notice' – and congratulate yourself every time you do.

Even when I am in my favourite wild places, I find it very challenging to remain aware of nature. I can go for a walk through a beautiful wood on a glorious sunny day, and find myself completely distracted by a constant stream of erratic thoughts and by struggling to connect with life around me. Moments like this can be intensely frustrating. But I have learnt that all I can do is notice my agitated mind, let it be and patiently keep bringing my attention back to the sunlight on the leaves, the sounds of the forest and the chirping birds.

Sometimes my mind will settle, at other times it won't. But no matter. The important thing is just to keep practising and enjoying any discoveries along the way. Remember that every time you notice, your awareness is growing a little more and you are opening up to a little more happiness and freedom in your life.

On Deeper Appreciation

The natural world can calm us, energize us and bring us happiness. If I have successfully encouraged you to seek out and invite a little bit more nature into your life for these reasons, then this book will have done its job. We all want to be happy and I cannot emphasize enough how important it is to simply enjoy our natural home. However, as we deepen our practice of mindfulness of the natural world, our awareness can begin to take us even further, towards a more intrinsic appreciation of nature.

What do I mean by intrinsic appreciation? Simply that appreciation of the natural world can be experienced on different levels. We can all appreciate nature as we feel uplifted by a sunny day, happier having seen colourful flowers in the park, invigorated after a swim in the sea or calmer after a long walk through the countryside. However, as we become more and more acquainted with nature's infinite tapestry of forms, patterns, colours, sensations, tunes, scents and textures, we may start to open up to a more intrinsic appreciation, where admiring the beauty of the natural world becomes an end in itself. We can begin to realize that we are no longer spending time with nature because it is good for us and has benefits for our well-being. Instead, we begin to look at the wonders of the natural world for their own sake, for no reason other than the delight of being in such close proximity with their beauty.

Falling in Love with Nature

This deeper appreciation is more akin to what we may call love. When I say love, I am referring to the feeling you have when you let go of your controlling mind and give in to being completely absorbed by the object of your awareness. Most of us have experienced, even unknowingly, how our sense of separate 'self' disappears when we are completely engaged in what we are doing or experiencing. We have all abandoned our sense of 'selves' to being captivated by the sight of a loved one, the sound of our favourite music, the story of an engaging book, or the trance of the rhythm of our morning run. As our sense of 'self' starts to dissolve, our minds tune in more wholly to what we are seeing and experiencing, and our habitual feelings and patterns of thought and behaviours become more spontaneous, open-ended and creative. It is as if we begin to let the world animate us as we animate it in return. In the case of music, for instance, you may literally begin to feel yourself animated into dance, movement or song in response to being absorbed by one of your favourite pieces.

MINDFULNESS PRACTICE

GIFTING FULL ATTENTION TO A FLOWER

❋

Find a flower in a meadow, a wood or simply in your garden. Allow your gaze to rest on the flower, its stem and its leaves. What shapes are the petals and leaves? What colour are they? Try to distinguish the subtlety of the various colours and their shades on the petals. Notice how these colours change depending on the lighting. Is there light passing through the petals or leaves? Then begin to notice any lines or patterns on the petals. What does the texture of the flower look like? What surface detail can you notice? Are the petals and leaves different? Explore the texture of the flower by running your finger over the surface. Is it smooth or rough? Do the leaves feel different from the petals? Bring your attention to your sense of smell. Notice your breath entering your nose and, as you bring the flower closer, become aware of the scent of the flower. Is it a sweet scent? As you engage with the flower, every time your mind wanders towards telling you stories about yourself or what you need to do next, notice how your mind may relate the flower or its scent to particular memories you have. Notice your sense of 'self' seeking your attention. Let these thoughts go, and softly return your attention to the flower. Enjoy exploring the flower with all your senses.

MINDFULNESS PRACTICE

A NATURE DAY

❋

Devote your full attention to the natural world for one whole day. Plan your trip for when you are sure to be able to avoid any distractions, and switch off your mobile phone for the day. Pack a notebook to record anything you notice or appreciate. If you need to travel to your chosen natural location, use public transport to reach your destination. This will allow you to begin your mindfulness practice during your journey. Become aware of plants, trees, animals, the air you are breathing. When you reach your destination and throughout the day keep all your senses aware of nature all around you. Write down anything specific that you appreciate – plants, birds, sounds of the sea or shapes of clouds. Try to describe the details you notice. Make sure that as well as walking, you stop from time to time to simply sit with nature and appreciate whatever you notice there. Look out for any specific details you may not have looked at before. You could spend your 'nature day' alone or share it with a friend.

The perceived separation between your sense of 'self' and the music disappears and you become an integral part of the music as the rhythm flows through your body.

You may argue that falling in love is a very personal thing, and maybe not everyone will feel love for the natural world. Nevertheless, we are all nature. If we love ourselves, then a love for all other living things is innate to us all. If we treasure life, we will treasure the natural world. And who doesn't treasure life?

Love at First Sight

We can all cultivate a deeper appreciation of nature. As we do so, we can start to relish simple things and take great pleasure in their beauty. Whether it is a flower in the wild, a bird foraging in the garden, a drop of dew on a blade of grass, an ant climbing up a brick wall or a nightingale singing melodically through the night, there is so much beauty in nature to enchant our minds and our hearts.

This profound appreciation of the beauty of nature may strike us in a single moment of awareness. This is what I would call 'falling in love at first sight'. The first time I felt a sense of intrinsic appreciation of nature was during my visit to the Chilean Lake District. In that instant of absolute satisfaction, my entire mind and body had tuned in to nature. I wasn't concerned about it being good for me or important for my well-being. I wasn't seeking companionship to calm my mind.

Developing an intrinsic appreciation of the natural world requires time and space.

It was enough just to be there, in that moment, with the wondrous beauty of the forests, the volcanoes, the lakes, the mountains, the birdsong. I felt as if I had transcended my sense of 'self' and all my needs and desires were satisfied.

Developing an intrinsic appreciation of the natural world requires time and space. For example, I find that if I go for a short mindful walk in nature when my mind is busy, it may take a while to settle and I find it difficult to engage fully with the wonders of life around me. However, on longer walks or during entire days spent among nature with no other distractions, I find I am more able to engage in appreciating it. See if you can put aside a couple of hours a week to go to a nature reserve, to the coast, to a wood or into the countryside and dedicate yourself to appreciating nature. Or take a 'mindfulness of the natural world' day trip to your favourite natural place. Make time to appreciate nature and give yourself to its undeniable charm.

THE BEAUTY OF LIFE

◆

We can all let the magnificence of nature touch us as we enquire deeper into its beauty. The potential for joy in the simple delight of appreciating natural beauty is in us all as an end in itself. To delve more profoundly into nature's marvels, we can cultivate mindfulness of the natural world through all our senses with increased involvement, intimacy, sympathy and detailed heartfelt appreciation.

I RECENTLY ATTENDED A SPEECH by Sir David Attenborough, which I will hold in my memory for ever. I felt highly privileged to have the opportunity to listen to a man who has inspired endless numbers of people, young and old, about the natural world. The sheer enthusiasm, wonder and passion in his voice were the undeniable expression of an utterly selfless appreciation of the intrinsic beauty of nature.

He vividly described his first experience of natural beauty, sixty years ago, with an energy and excitement that made it sound like it was only yesterday. He recounted the story of when he saw the 'astonishing beauty, complexity and wonder of the natural world' for the first time. He had just stepped out of an old aircraft onto a grass airstrip on the coast of West Africa. As he stood on the airstrip, he looked around him with a sense of wonder. He was gifted at once with a view of wonderful scarlet-coloured hibiscus flowers, beautiful tropical butterflies, a touch-sensitive mimosa plant and a chameleon.

It was his first experience of the diversity of the life of the tropical rainforest and even the airstrip he had landed on was teeming with life. He exclaimed that this moment was for him the 'revelation of how miraculous the natural world can be' and how this has never ceased to affect him. I remember noticing how the tone of his voice was emptied of any sense of personal gain from the scene. Rather, he was an integral part of the wonder he was experiencing.

Memory of a Cuban Sunrise

I too have had the privilege of being intimately immersed in breathtaking natural beauty on a number of occasions. I remember once feeling totally absorbed by the appreciation of a particularly awe-inspiring view when I was travelling in Cuba. I had risen at dawn. I crept out onto the porch of the house to avoid waking my friend in the room next door. I glanced across at the view of dome-shaped isolated limestone hills covered in dense, vividly green vegetation, dominating a vast landscape of tobacco fields and red farmlands. What a view to wake up to.

My initial glance quickly turned into a gaze, captivated by the amazing beauty of the sight. A natural ethereal aura of white mist softly floated in the air, draping the rolling fields in a gauzy veil of tranquillity. Ghostly silhouettes of palm trees punctuated the landscape's mosaic of hazy green and red. Gigantic grey fluffy clouds emerged from behind the domes and were gradually lit up from beneath into a soft orange glow. The stillness of the scene generated by the mist married with the majesty of the domes into a magnificent sight. At intervals, a bird would timidly begin to sing, seemingly afraid to disturb the peace of the moment. I felt as if, like me, all other living things were absorbed into the scene and had become an integral part of it. The orange glow was getting brighter by the minute as the sun illuminated the landscape. The purity and freshness of the morning air perfectly complemented the exquisite spectacle.

I didn't realize until afterwards, but my sense of 'self' was absent. I was simply absorbed by the intrinsic wonder of the view and intimately engulfed in a deep contemplation of the pure grace and delicate beauty of nature. I was an integral part of the scene. I didn't dare to speak out loud, not even a whisper. I waited until the rest of the life around me had agreed that it was time to transform the landscape into the glory of a new day.

Encounter with a Magpie

Bringing our attention more closely to familiar sights of nature enables us to discover and appreciate their detail. The black-billed magpie, common throughout most of Eurasia, is widespread in suburban areas and in the countryside. I have seen a magpie on most days of my life, yet I usually tend to dismiss them as 'common black-and-white birds'. One day, I was sitting on a bench in a city park when a magpie hopped in front of me. Rather than dismissing it and returning to my book, I decided to give the bird my full attention. I was struck by the beauty of the glossy velvety-black of his head, neck and bill. The intense darkness of his plumage contrasted perfectly with the clean white of his belly and shoulders. I then noticed a striking metallic blue and green sheen each side of his body. This sheen shone out gloriously from the rest of his black and white plumage as it shimmered in the sunlight. I examined his long graduated black tail. He carefully lifted it off the ground as he walked and hopped from one side to the other, as if to protect a precious ornament. Occasionally, as he fluttered his wings, I caught a glimpse of the pure white of the inner webs of his wings.

The magpie continued to hop around in front of me for a few minutes, every so often tilting his head to one side with a glint of intelligence in his eye. He displayed a shy but confident character, seemingly relaxed in my presence, albeit maintaining a safe distance. A few seconds later, he flew up to sit on the branch of a nearby tree. As he took off, his wings opened up in perfect symmetry into two beautiful fans and more colours were revealed to me. His tail glistened into iridescent bronze and green and the blue colour of the wings was enhanced with the addition of shiny green and purple reflections. What a wonderful sight! In a instant of appreciation, I felt as if the bird and I had shared a moment of life.

Take a closer look sometimes at any common birds you see. Whether it is a sparrow, a pigeon or a crow, gift them with your attention. Engage with the beauty of their plumage, their movements and their song. You will be sure to discover unexpected marvels you have never been aware of before.

There is so much life around us that we can admire. Take some time in your life to give yourself freely to this beauty, with no expectation or aim. See if from time to time you can merely see nature for its own sake. Cultivate a gentle openness, childish exploration and playfulness when you look at nature, and prepare to receive anything that it may gift you along the way.

Inspired by Life

As we deepen appreciation of the world around us and tune in to life, our conscious minds can become our most precious asset. The more mindful we become of the natural world, the more we may begin to let go of the separation between our 'selves' and nature, as nature begins to animate and move us. In turn, we can begin to animate the world and participate with our full potential in the unfolding of life.

The beauty of the natural world has inspired humans ever since we first evolved on the planet. It is likely that art first appeared in our evolutionary history about 30,000 years ago, around the same time as we developed and used tools. A number of wonderful prehistoric paintings have been discovered in caves, depicting symbolic images of dangerous or hunted animals with mythological features galloping across the murals. These are the first records of our species being inspired to create art following observation of the natural world. Since then, a deep awareness of nature's beauty has inspired infinite numbers of artists, poets, musicians, writers and scientists. It has moved many of them to draw, paint, write, compose, understand and model the natural world for centuries. Expression of emotions related to experiences of the natural world is the second most prominent source of inspiration for artists after romantic love.

Nature in Art...

Visual art has taken inspiration from nature ever since those first prehistoric cave paintings. Have you ever walked through an art gallery without seeing any paintings depicting nature? The French impressionist Claude Monet, famous for his beautiful paintings of water lilies in his garden at Giverny, said that nature was his primary source of inspiration. Most of his paintings represent the daily and seasonal variations in colour,

---

If you truly love Nature,

you will find beauty everywhere.

VINCENT VAN GOGH (1853–90)
DUTCH POST-IMPRESSIONIST PAINTER

---

light and shape of the natural world. The Dutch painter Vincent van Gogh also painted in the open air. His art is an astonishing illustration of how a deep appreciation of the natural world can begin to move and animate our experience. Through his paintings of olive trees, flowers and other landscapes, van Gogh expressed how his emotions were affected and moved by the powers of the natural world. These feelings were an integral part of his artistic expression and he wanted his art to reflect his connection with the sacredness of nature.

...In Music

A number of musical composers have also been inspired by the natural world. As a pianist, one of my favourite composers is Claude Debussy. His great talent resides in the expression of visual scenes of nature through musical composition. In fact, he took much of his inspiration from impressionist paintings. To me, the dreamy, light, colourful, vague, free-flowing music in his compositions such as 'Arabesques' and 'Clair de Lune' perfectly depicts the pure and ever-changing beauty of the natural world.

Unsurprisingly, birdsong, the music of the natural world, has inspired a great number of composers. In particular, the French composer and ornithologist Olivier Messiaen wove inspiration from birdsong into most of his works. He saw birdsong as music in itself, as well as a source of inspiration and fascination. One of his most famous compositions is the

---

In melancholy moments, when my uselessness is
brutally revealed to me, what else is there to do
except search for the true face of Nature, forgotten
somewhere in the forest, in the fields, in the mountains,
on the seashore, among the birds? For me, it is here that
music lives: music that is free, anonymous, improvised.

OLIVIER MESSIAEN (1908–92)
FRENCH COMPOSER & ORNITHOLOGIST

'Réveil des Oiseaux' (awakening of the birds), in which he
conveys his experiences of listening to the songs of birds in
south-west France, including nightingales, little owls, wood-
larks, warblers and many others. He uses the different musical
instruments to express the colours and tones of the various
birdsongs and marries them into a wonderful composition for
piano and orchestra. The work reflects the songs of birds from
midnight to midday, interrupted by two lengthy silences, at
dawn and noon.

The composer Ludwig van Beethoven is also known to have
been deeply inspired by the natural world. He had a great love
of nature, enjoying long walks in the country so much that he
refused to take an umbrella with him, in order to embrace
downpours of heavy rain. His sixth symphony, the 'Pastoral',
was inspired by his deep love of nature. Through this composition, he expresses his feelings about how the beauty and power

of natural elements such as flowing water and tremendous thunderstorms moved him. Some say that when he composed the second movement, 'By the Brook', the buntings, nightingales and cuckoos had been 'composing along with him'. As he immersed himself in the natural world, it was as if nature was fully participating in his art, and he was an integral player in the symphony of life around him.

...And in Literature & Science

So many writers and poets have been inspired by nature. From the epic works of ancient Greek poets to Basho's three-line haikus and beyond, thousands of poets and writers have translated their experience into words and verse. Of course, great scientists such as Newton, Einstein and Darwin were also fuelled by their passionate observation of the natural world to constantly improve their understanding, prediction and modelling of its functioning.

These wonderful creations from the worlds of art and science, resulting from the expression of human appreciation of the rest of the natural world, are truly mind-blowing.

◆

Look deep into nature
and you will understand everything.

ALBERT EINSTEIN (1879–1955)
THEORETICAL PHYSICIST

◆

Opening Up to Nature through Art & Science

As we become more acquainted with our minds by increasing our awareness of our thoughts and emotions through the practice of mindfulness, we can learn to appreciate and pay more attention to our experiences in the world. Our impressively complex minds can then become the source of prodigious creativity. Tuning our minds in to life and allowing the natural world to animate our experience and inspire us to express our perceptions of it is one of the truly wonderful ways in which we can all share and celebrate the intrinsic beauty of our natural home.

Interestingly, the practice of art and science can, in turn, act as excellent entry points to deepening our mindfulness of the natural world. If you enjoy painting, or writing, or composing music, see if you can use these skills to deepen your awareness of nature. Do you like taking photographs? Taking a camera out into nature is a great way to encourage us to pay more attention to what we see and to discover and appreciate natural beauty. If you have a busy mind that finds it difficult to connect with the sights you encounter on your walk, using your camera to look out for colours, patterns, shades of light and movement could be a brilliant way to channel your awareness of them.

Whatever you love doing, see if you can use the creative activities you enjoy in your everyday life to connect more often and more deeply with the beauty of nature.

MINDFULNESS PRACTICE

MINDFUL PHOTOGRAPHY

✻

Taking photographs of the natural world – capturing what we see that interests us, balancing light and composition, focusing on colour and form – can help deepen our appreciation of the natural world. Looking at the photos we have taken afterwards can reveal new detail, reflections, colours and elements of beauty. When out on a walk, become aware of what is around you. Look at your subject from different angles and notice how the colour, light, contrast and composition change. Take photos from these different angles. Take close-ups and more distant shots: individual flower-heads or the whole meadow mix of flowers and grasses; sunlight illuminating fresh spring leaves or the whole verdant scene of a woodland. Do your photos reflect what you saw, what originally attracted your attention, or do they reveal new colours, shapes or textures that you were not aware of?

NATURAL WISDOM

We can all learn a lot from nature about how to live our lives. Why might this be? Nature holds all the secrets and wonders of life. It creates, sustains and orchestrates all living things. So if we want to know more about living, let's look at life!

T HE STORIES IN OUR MINDS may convince us that we know how best to live our lives. They may tell us that 'To live a successful life, you must make sure you are in control of everything', 'I might as well give up if I'm going to have to wait that long' or 'The more money I have, the happier I will be'. In my experience, the majority of these stories are untrue. Trying to control everything causes me a lot of frustration and suffering. Giving up too quickly can lead to missed opportunities. What I do always affects other people in some way, and having more money has never made me feel happier.

So what does the natural world have to teach us about life? Well, firstly, there is a difference between learning *about*

Come forth into the light of things,

let Nature be your teacher.

WILLIAM WORDSWORTH (1770–1850)
ENGLISH ROMANTIC POET

nature and learning *from* nature. Most of our conventional learning related to the natural world is focused on learning *about* nature. We study the rest of nature as if separate from us with the aim of ensuring that we can understand it, organize it, control it and make use of it. Learning *from* nature is completely different. In order to learn *from* nature, we need to learn to let go of our separation from it. We need to be in it.

Lessons from the Natural World

During his two-year experiment living a simple life in the woods, Henry David Thoreau sought to learn about the truths of life, and his education was based on one main thing: awareness of all of his senses. Instead of learning about nature, he bathed in the natural world and allowed himself to be infused with the truths and wisdom of life. Learning from nature is fully tuning in to nature with complete openness and reflecting on whatever it may have to teach us.

Of course, we aren't all going to head out and build a little hut in the woods to live in the sole company of nature for two years like Thoreau. However, as we spend longer contemplating the natural world, we may catch glimpses of insight into its infinite wisdom. Personally, there are four main things I have learnt from mindfulness of the natural world: acceptance, patience, impermanence and interconnectedness. These are things nature teaches me about a little more each day and they can greatly enhance our lives.

Acceptance

I was once lucky enough to take part in a wildlife safari in the African savannah. The vast, open, arid and dusty plains extended all the way to the horizon in a landscape that seemed devoid of life. My throat was feeling extremely dry and I had forgotten to bring my water bottle. I noticed my mind frustratingly wishing for an immediate drink to quench my thirst. Just as I began to let this uncomfortable feeling distract me, the safari guide stopped the truck: 'Elephants on our right.' A herd of elephants was walking in single file, parallel to our direction of travel. They walked slowly onwards in the midday heat and the silence of their footsteps against the dusty ground amazed me, considering their impressive size. Our guide explained that they were on their way to seek water. 'There are very few water holes where elephants live, but the older members of the herd know where they are. It could take them a few days to make it to the nearest river bank or lake in this unbearable heat,' he said.

See if you can perceive acceptance in the natural world.

Listening to this, my own thirst seemed less important. I knew I would be rehydrated once I returned to the camp, within a matter of an hour or so. As I brought my attention back to these wonderful creatures, I was struck by their acceptance of their situation. As I engaged in this contemplation, my attention was drawn to their eyes. Their expression revealed a sense of beautiful innocence, gentleness and acceptance, which touched me profoundly. They courageously walked on through the midday heat in order to satisfy this simple necessity of life: finding water.

When I see trees growing on the edge of cliffs against the odds of the wind and cold, birds puffing up their feathers to protect themselves from the cold in the winter, and wild flowers growing alongside railway lines, I am filled with a sense of humility. I see that the rest of the natural world doesn't complain or resist the events of life over which it has no control. Learning to accept the things we can't change in our lives, such as painful emotions, suffering, loss and external events that hinder our goals, is at the heart of allowing greater contentment into our lives. Having the courage to take action to change the things we can alter is also essential if we want to create a happier life for ourselves and others. See if you can perceive acceptance in the natural world and become aware of where acceptance may reduce unnecessary suffering in your own life.

◆

Grant me the serenity to accept the things I
cannot change, the courage to change the things I can
and the wisdom to know the difference.

REINHOLD NIEBUHR (1892–1971)
AMERICAN THEOLOGIAN

◆

Patience

I remember once sitting by a slow-flowing river in the tropics. On a leafless branch overhanging the river, a kingfisher sat
staring into the distance with his bright copper chest shimmering in the sunlight. Suddenly, he jolted his head downwards
and stared, motionless, at the water below. From this high
vantage point, the bird could spy the movements of fish swimming below him. He kept his body and head completely still.
The bird remained fixed on the same spot for what felt to me
like an eternity. His bright white collar glared in the sunshine,
stark against the dark green feathers of his small body. He sat
undisturbed, focused and ready to strike. The heat of the sun
was beating down on his head as well as on mine. He didn't
seem to mind, whereas I felt an immediate desire to retreat to
the shade. Out of the corner of my eye I saw a cormorant
stretch out its wings to dry them in the heat of the sun. The
kingfisher waited. I remember shifting my legs restlessly
while swatting the mosquitoes that were attacking my bare
skin. I watched an egret fly gracefully just above the water. I
glanced back at the kingfisher. He was still waiting. I felt my
impatience to witness the thrilling sight of his strike starkly

---

Adopt the pace of nature, her secret is patience.

RALPH WALDO EMERSON (1803–82)
AMERICAN ESSAYIST, POET & LEADER OF THE TRANSCENDENTAL MOVEMENT

---

contrasted with the composure of the bird in the tropical sunshine. I became aware of my mind refusing the slow passing of time. I gazed back at the kingfisher, still patiently waiting for the opportune moment to catch his late-morning meal.

In the natural world, events happen in their own time and there is no pressure to achieve things faster than necessary. Nature doesn't surrender on a whim and knows how to take its time to build. A tree growing from a seedling or a lion stalking its prey reveals the value of patience. Try to bring nature's patience to mind in your own life. See if you can slow down occasionally. Strive to give people and activities your full attention, for the length of time they deserve and need. Remember that in order to create a good piece of work, a good relationship or allow ourselves to experience our emotions as they come and go, we need to cultivate a kindly sense of patience towards ourselves and others.

Impermanence

When I sit by a river, staring at the patterns on its surface, I am reminded that, despite the fact that the river is a constant feature of the landscape, the water I am seeing is always different. Indeed, as Heraclitus pointed out, you can 'never swim in the same river twice'.

This is a perfect illustration of the reality of impermanence. When we accept impermanence as an integral part of life, we feel freer and happier. The reality of impermanence means that whatever is going on in our lives, the present moment we are in is immensely precious. We are alive right now, and this moment, as it is, will never return again, so let's appreciate it. The reality of impermanence also makes everything possible. Without impermanence, a seed would never grow into a tree and an embryo would never grow into an adult human being. Practising mindfulness of our thoughts and emotions also gives us insight into impermanence. Pleasurable and painful thoughts and emotions will come and go all the time. We can't hold on to them, push them away or make them stay with us for ever. All we can do is accept them. And remember that we can be comforted by the fact that they will always be changing.

Interconnectedness

I once sat contemplating a flowering bush outside my window. The delicate pink flowers were overwhelmed by the to-ing and fro-ing of honeybees hovering from flower to flower, collecting nectar and carrying pollen. This bustling community of life was a simple joy to watch. As I contemplated the scene in the morning sunshine, I began to ponder on how the rest of life was involved. The bush had been nurtured by rain, sunshine and nutrients in the soil. Its growth had then resulted in its branches and flowers. The production of nectar by the flowers enticed the bees to visit them, collecting sweet nectar and pollen to take back to their hive. They would then deposit

Nothing endures but change.

HERACLITUS (C.535–C.475 BCE)
GREEK PHILOSOPHER

---

the nectar in the honeycomb cells and feed the pollen to their growing young larvae. The heat in the hive circulated by the bees beating their wings would evaporate the excess water from the nectar in the honeycomb, transforming it into honey. Simultaneously, as they journeyed from one flower to the next, the bees also transferred pollen between them on their tiny hairy bodies. The transferred pollen then led to the production of a next generation of the plant. I was astonished by how much of what I was seeing was dependent, and related to so many other parts of the natural world.

If you pay attention to anything that is alive, you will see that it is intimately linked to the rest of nature. The importance of interconnectedness also applies to our everyday lives. Notice how what you do or say impacts on other people's lives. Everywhere, life is primarily about connections and relationships with others. See how encouraging compassion, communication and cooperation in everyday life leads to greater results than resigning yourself to isolation and generating conflict. Understanding that we can't live under the illusion that we are entirely separate from the rest of the world around us is important for our own well-being as well

Pull a thread here and you'll find it's
attached to the rest of the world.

NADEEM ASLAM (B.1966)
BRITISH-PAKISTANI NOVELIST

as for the well-being of the rest of life on Earth. Our entire lives, the food we eat, the clothes we own, the activities we engage in, the people we spend time with, all depend on developing and nurturing infinite numbers of connections. See if you can become more aware of these connections in your everyday life.

A New Understanding of Life

As we deepen our awareness and appreciation of the boundless beauty and wisdom of nature, and continue to let go of our sense of separated 'self', we may begin to recognize that we are not masters or appointed stewards of the universe, but merely a part of nature. We may then start to *feel* our innate intimacy and identification with the natural world.

This understanding of life is the essence of what is now called deep ecology. Deep ecology, as coined by the Norwegian environmental philosopher Arne Naess, is the understanding that the natural world did not come to exist as a resource and playground for us human beings. Rather, it is an awesomely complex web of interconnected diverse life forms, which all have intrinsic value and all play an important part in the symphony of life. This value does not depend on how useful it is to us, or on whether it can be exploited in some way. It is not an economic value. It is an inherent value attributed to all of life. If we take this view, then no life form is inherently more important, superior or valuable than any other. Mahatma Gandhi is known to have had a similar view of the world as he worked to encourage a solidarity and respect for all forms of life.

Have you ever had moments in your life when you felt an unexpected sense of wordless and thoughtless meaning or understanding? It might have been during a simple day at work over a problem you were trying to solve, while standing on top of a mountain looking down into a valley or maybe when going through intense pain or loss in your life when a loved one has passed away. At times like these, everything around you may seem to take on a whole new meaning. These revelations of insight take us by surprise. We can't engineer them or search for them. But we can remain open to them.

In terms of the natural world, moments of revelation of the unity of life can be experienced by us all. This was the essence of my Chilean experience and I hope that, as we continue to deepen our awareness of nature, we may all encounter these moments in our lives.

CHAPTER FIVE

PROTECTING THE LIFE WE LOVE

*Understanding the unity of life has
important consequences for our own happiness,
and for our relationship with the rest of the natural
world. A feeling of intimate identification with all
living things naturally leads us to an attitude of
compassion and loving kindness towards all life.
We then more naturally take action that avoids
deliberately causing suffering to the rest of the
natural world. At whatever level we appreciate
nature, the most important thing is to experience
and enjoy it in every way we can. If we love the
natural world, we are more likely to take action
to ensure its protection in the context of the
current environmental crisis.*

IN TOUCH WITH THE UNITY OF LIFE

◆

As we expand our awareness towards the rest of nature, we gain an uplifting feeling of being part of something much greater than ourselves, a genuine sense of intimacy with all life. The potential for this heartfelt insight into nature lies within us all. We just need to keep paying attention to the natural world, with our minds and hearts ready to receive.

B UT WHY IS THE EXPERIENCE of feeling part of the unity of life so important? Why is it essential for us to reconnect with the undeniable reality that we are not separate from the rest of nature? We considered earlier how our minds have created a separation between our sense of permanent 'self' and our bodies, as well as between our sense of 'self' and nature, and thus separated and isolated us in our experience of life. But this separation isn't a reflection of the reality of our experience. This is why mindfulness of both our experience and our natural home is vital for anyone who wants to reconnect with life. Discovering that, in fact, we are fundamentally one with the rest of life is at the heart of alleviating suffering for ourselves and for our fellow creatures. Despite what our minds may tell us, we don't exist without the rest of the natural world. We never have done so and we never will.

We don't exist without the rest of the natural world.

Happiness in Unity

The Vietnamese Buddhist monk Thich Nhat Hanh said, 'We are here to awaken from our illusion of separateness.' We all want to be happy, and feeling a sense of unity and belonging is essential to our happiness. Feeling part of something is an important aspiration that we have as human beings – part of a relationship, a family, a group of friends, a sports team, a choir or just part of an experience, like when we are totally absorbed in a piece of music or immersed in the adventures of a book. Feeling connected to life and to other people makes us feel good.

In a world where separation and isolation are becoming part of our modern culture, and where our minds are filled with stories advocating the importance of speed, success, money and productivity, mindfulness of the natural world has never been more important for our well-being. As we deepen our appreciation of nature towards an understanding of the unity of life, we begin to awaken to the fact that our separation, our loneliness and our quest for meaning are all just constructs of the mind.

When we get in touch with the unified nature of creation, we begin to open up to the fact that we are an integral part of the Tree of Life. We get back in touch with ourselves and find that we are not separated and isolated. Beyond the realms of our minds, we are alive in our bodies, at every moment, an integral cog in the world around us.

Finding Our True Self

We have seen how mindfulness of our thoughts, emotions and direct experience of life takes us out of our minds and into real living through our senses. If we *are* nature, then a deeper connection to nature encourages a deeper connection with our true selves. As we let go of the rule of our minds and immerse ourselves in life, we are filled with a sense of freedom, allowing us to become our authentic selves. Like all living things, we begin to actively participate in a wonderful, ever-changing stage of life. When we start to experience this, our purpose can be found in the simple experience of being alive, at each moment.

Start to think about all other plants and animals you come across as part of your natural family. Connect with them as often as you can in all the ways we have explored. Nature is a home to us all. Through the practice of mindfulness, cultivate a relationship with the natural world. In the same way that you would find cosiness in your own house, you will find comfort, belonging and freedom in the company of nature.

Friends with the Rest of Life

The understanding of the unity of life also has important effects on our relationship with all other living things. One of its main consequences is that we start to see that our species is not essentially superior to any other species on the planet. Instead, humans are just a small branch in the tree of life, a very recently evolved species among a marvellous array of other amazing creatures. Of course, we have a number of special characteristics that other species don't have – larger brains, conscious thought, awareness of complex emotions and a great capacity to create and innovate. We are an astonishing life form in many ways. But can we breathe under water like a fish? Can we fly like the birds? Can we use light and transform it into energy for life like the trees? No. All plants and animals have characteristics that suit their individual lifestyles. Dolphins have the capacity to echo-locate other animals and objects in their aquatic environment. Cuttlefish can instantly become invisible by perfectly mimicking background colours and patterns as they travel across the ocean floor. Desert plants can retain water in order to survive in their arid habitat.

The point is that all life forms display their own brilliance in the context of the environment they live in. Every individual of every species on the planet is playing its own part in the unfolding of the totality of life. Every life form is valuable in its own way and this is what makes the natural world so awe-inspiring and diverse. We all have a right to be alive and, of course, humans have a unique place in the universe; but so do other mammals, insects, fungi, bacteria, fish, reptiles, amphibians, rivers, mountains and rocks. As we learn to appreciate the wonder in nature's endless creativity of forms, we will start to feel the uplifting privilege of being part of it.

DEVELOPING GRATITUDE

✳

Every evening, write a list of five things in nature that you noticed that day and feel grateful for. It could be the birds singing as you step out of your house in the morning; the sun shining; the blossom on the trees; a butterfly; the snow; the wind in the trees. Or it might be the apple you ate at lunchtime, the water you were drinking throughout the day or simply the air you are breathing. As you make the list, bring these appreciative thoughts to mind. Say to yourself, 'I appreciated the sun shining, I appreciated that beautiful butterfly, I am grateful for the air I am breathing that keeps me alive.' Notice how bringing them to mind makes you feel. Notice any changes in your body. Appreciative thoughts are good for us. Being grateful makes us feel happier, more relaxed and improves our well-being.

Respect & Reverence

As we begin to feel part of the web of life, our sense of control and ownership of nature is replaced by a natural sentiment of innate respect and reverence for all living things. We see that, despite what our minds have convinced us of, we are not the masters of life. We begin to relinquish our sense of control over nature and immerse ourselves into it with greater humility. The natural world is constantly revealing to us that we can't control it. Think about the weather, natural disasters, the planet's climate, the emergence of life and the existence of death. We have no true power over any of these. We have done a convincing job of enacting the story that 'nature belongs to us', by changing and adapting our environments to try to master nature's ways. But there are some indisputable realities of the natural world, such as the interconnectedness and impermanence of all of life, that we will never be able to override without causing universal suffering.

Seeing the unity of life leads to an understanding that we are not the pinnacle of evolution. Our consciousness and larger brains do not equate with us being more advanced than other life forms. They are just characteristics we display, as wonderful as the ability elephants have to hear the lowest-frequency sounds or the navigational skills of migratory birds. Why would having a more complex brain and experience of life make us intrinsically better than any other species? We are merely another participating thread in the web of life.

A Shared Identity

Perhaps the most important consequence of getting in touch with the oneness of life is the emergence of a sense of intimacy and identification with other life forms. As we cease to see the rest of the natural world as a resource for us to exploit and instead develop a greater awareness of it, it becomes a part of us, which we identify with and appreciate. In this light, other life forms become our friends. Of course, I'm not expecting us to start to socialize with the ants and the bees and engage in conversation with the trees – by friends, I mean that we start looking at other plants and animals as our equals. We start to feel a sense of mutuality and reciprocity in our relationship with them. We appreciate everything we receive from nature as a momentary gift. Air, water, sunshine, encounters with other plants and animals are all gifts of nature. The natural world becomes something to be appreciated, valued and celebrated, rather than something to be tamed and exploited to satisfy our every desire.

Appreciating other species as friends means that we develop a sense of compassion for them. Every one of us wants to be happy and free from suffering. We naturally want the same for our close family and friends and all the people we care for. Why is this? Because through our feelings of love for them, we empathize with them, appreciate them and consequently wish them well. Would you ever deliberately cause harm or pain to any of the people you love? If you have a cat

or a dog as a pet, would you ever hurt them on purpose? Of course you wouldn't.

The more you get to know other people in your life, the more you realize that we all have similar concerns, worries, frustrations and desires for contentment, meaning and peace in our lives. Even those who seem perfectly happy, successful and content from the outside experience problems, fears and uncertainties. We all know what it is to feel pain, loss, stress and suffering. Consequently, we naturally want to prevent our loved ones from being the subject of any form of harm. Through love of other people, we can empathize with their happiness, sadness, pleasure and pain. Our love and deep appreciation of them leads to the disappearance of our separate sense of 'self'. We become animated by how they are feeling. We react by wanting to share in their joy, by helping them when they are feeling down or by reminding them of our love when they are going through a difficult time.

Extending Compassion to the Natural World

Mindfulness of the natural world and feeling our connection with the rest of life can lead us to naturally extend this feeling of compassion beyond other human beings, to all life. You might say that other forms of life do not share our aspirations when it comes to what we call happiness. They are not seeking deep feelings of meaning or purpose in their lives. They have different requirements for their well-being. Nevertheless, no

◆

Every living being is connected intimately, and from
this intimacy follows capacity of identification and as its
natural consequences, practice of non-violence.

ARNE NAESS (1912–2009)
NORWEGIAN PHILOSOPHER

◆

sentient being wants to suffer, and a love for nature leads to a
natural desire to avoid inflicting suffering on it. No other species on Earth apart from ours causes suffering to others,
unless their life depends on it. Only our species lives in conflict with nature, exploiting it deliberately; but if we start to
look at our natural home as our friend, our relationship with
it becomes more of a partnership than a conflict. Just remember that nature gives us what we most value: our lives.

How Is Nature Feeling?

Next time you are walking out in nature with a friend, stop
for a second and think to yourself: 'How is the world around
me experiencing this scene?' Remind yourself that you are
not the only living thing there, experiencing that moment.
Consider how your friend may be feeling. What thoughts
might be going through their mind? You could even ask them.
Ask them what they are aware of in their surroundings. Ask
them which aspects of the walk they are enjoying. How is that
different from your experience?

You can also think about how any birds you can see or hear may be living at this moment. What might their perception be of you? Could there be any other animals around that you are not aware of? How might they be experiencing this instant? There may be insects in the undergrowth or flying around you. What is their take on the world?

You may argue that they are probably not feeling much. This may be true, but they still have a perception of the world that is different from yours. They can still sense the world around them. Think about any challenges they may have in their lives, like seeking food or avoiding predators. Think about some of the things in their lives that might be good for them. Consider whether some animals may even take pleasure in some aspects of life. Birds may enjoy singing. Young mammals may enjoy chasing each other and playing in the sunshine. Predators may feel a sense of satisfaction as they tuck into a meal they have spent time and energy catching.

Loving Kindness

Most sentient forms of life will 'experience' life at some level – and why should their experience be less worthy than ours? They too live in avoidance of pain, death, hunger and suffering. They all evolved with the sole challenge of staying alive and reproducing. In order to do this, they too try to enhance their health and well-being and avoid things that will harm them. See if you can occasionally engage with this sense of intimate appreciation, concern and compassion for all living things. Bring to mind the fact that, like you, they are also alive and wanting to avoid suffering.

The Buddha called this sort of friendship or compassion for all living beings 'metta' – which translates as 'loving kindness'. He said that compassion begins with ourselves. We start by wishing ourselves to be well, happy and free from suffering. When we become accepting, warmer and kinder towards ourselves and our experience of life, we are naturally kinder to others. We can then expand this warmth and kindness towards our family, friends, people we may not know, people we may not like and all living things. The development of loving kindness is a demanding practice that requires time. However, see if you can cultivate a bit of loving kindness towards yourself, other people in your life and the natural world around you every day. As we keep practising, we begin to see beyond what is best for ourselves, or for other people, towards what is good for all life that is affected by our actions. Loving kindness for all life on Earth is the ultimate result of the deepest understanding of the unity of life.

Appreciation of the interconnectedness of life leads us to an understanding that being in conflict with nature is being in conflict with our own well-being. The practice of mindfulness of the natural world changes our relationship with ourselves and with the rest of life, moving towards one of harmony and connection. We all have the innate capacity to awaken to this

MINDFULNESS PRACTICE

CULTIVATING KINDNESS & COMPASSION FOR LIFE

❋

The cultivation of 'metta' is a popular form of Buddhist meditation. 'Metta' is a Pali word meaning loving-kindness or friendliness. See if you can cultivate it in your everyday life.

• Sit comfortably and feel your breath for a few moments. Notice how your heart area feels, and accept whatever you find without trying to change it. After a few minutes, say kindly to yourself: 'May I be happy, may I be well.' Notice any self-critical thoughts you may have and let them go as you return to awareness of your heart area.

• Once you have done this for a few minutes, bring to mind one after the other: a close friend, a person you have seen but feel neutral about and a person you find a little difficult. Become aware that they also want to be happy but have their own difficulties in life. Spend a few minutes bringing each of these people to mind, cultivating a feeling of kindness towards them. For each of them, say to yourself: 'May they be well, may they be happy.' Don't worry if nothing happens; there is no right or wrong way to feel. Now extend the feeling out towards all living things such as birds, mammals, insects and plants. Remind yourself that they too want to be alive, happy and free from suffering.

new understanding of life. In doing so, we can invite greater feelings of appreciation, kindness, happiness and well-being into our lives. As well as being important for our personal happiness, this is also a vital realization when it comes to the environmental crisis our planet is facing today.

PROTECTING WHAT WE LOVE

◆

Think for a moment of all that you love and appreciate in your life. Now imagine how you would feel if it were taken from you. You would do something about it, wouldn't you? This is a natural reaction. People protect what they love. We have a natural desire to care for the people and things we value and maintain them in our lives. We need no persuasion to do so.

IT IS COMMONLY AGREED that, given the crisis our planet is facing, the key to sustainably protecting the rapidly declining natural world in the long term lies in a change in our behaviour. However, when you hear about how many species are becoming extinct, how the rain forests are being cut down, how climate change is going to affect the whole planet and how life in the oceans is being over-exploited, do you feel inspired to take action? If anything, thinking about all of these problems makes me feel like hiding away and distancing myself from them. This is because we rarely take positive action out of fear. Fear causes us to run away from problems.

Of course, the atrocity of what we are doing to the planet is undeniably real and there are issues we need to face up to. However, knowledge of these problems will never be the source of inspiration that gives us the genuine will to take action to protect our home. When you read economic arguments in the media about the need to slow down climate change, protect the forests and sources of water, save energy and reduce waste, do you feel driven to take action? They are all perfectly sound, rational arguments in the context of today's world and they are important considerations. However, they are not sufficient. No amount of information and intellectual knowledge alone will change our behaviour and our relationship with nature. Why would we take action to protect something we don't *feel* anything about?

Only a genuine love for the natural world will give us the desire to care for and protect it. The American author and scientist Aldo Leopold, influential in the development of the modern environmental movement, wrote: 'We can only be ethical in relation to something that we can feel, understand, love or otherwise have faith in.' As I hope I have shown you, nature is part of us and so we all have this innate affection for

---

People protect what they love.

JACQUES COUSTEAU (1910–97)
FRENCH CONSERVATIONIST & WRITER

We can only be ethical in relation to something that we
can feel, understand, love or otherwise have faith in.

ALDO LEOPOLD (1887–1948)
AMERICAN WRITER & ENVIRONMENTALIST

---

it within us. If we recognize that the natural world is essential
to our well-being and happiness, addressing the environmental crisis becomes a natural course of action, rather than a
duty imposed upon us. Taking action to protect the natural
world is no longer about being told to make drastic changes
in our lives, use less energy, recycle and consume less. Instead,
it becomes more about listening to what our hearts are telling
us and protecting something that matters to us.

From the Heart

In 2009, the Nature Conservancy published the results of a
survey that asked supporters of wildlife conservation why
they cared about the natural world. Interestingly, the results
showed that their love of nature originated in an inspirational
experience of it at some point in their lives. They didn't take
action to protect the natural world because scientific papers
convinced them of its economic value, or because they had
seen graphs representing predictions of what the planet's climate might look like in a hundred years' time. These rational
arguments merely serve to support a passion for the natural

world they feel in their hearts. All of my friends and colleagues who work in the field of nature conservation have a
similar passion for the natural world.

My travels in the Chilean Lake District were my source of
inspiration that led me to devote my life to appreciating and
protecting the natural world. I don't work for an international conservation organization because I feel I'm 'doing
something good' or because 'I should'. Instead, it was the
unforgettable experience of breathing in the fresh air of the
temperate rainforests, listening to the fast-flowing rivers and
marvelling at awe-inspiring views of snow-capped volcanoes
that led me along this career path. I fell in love with the natural
world and nothing else felt more 'right' than dedicating my
life to contributing to its protection. I was driven by a passion
that came not from my thinking mind but from my heart.

Inspiring the Next Generation

This is another reason why getting our children back into
nature is vital for the future of the planet. They will have
plenty of time to learn about the plight of the rainforests and
the rise of sea levels. But more importantly, it is essential that
they have a direct, fun, exploratory experience of the natural
world first. Simply educating them about the environmental
crisis is more likely to send them straight indoors to watch
television and forget all about it. If they don't love nature,
why would they fight for it later on?

MINDFULNESS & THE NATURAL WORLD

It is for all these reasons that mindfulness of the natural world is essential to support its protection. How can we connect with our innate love for the natural world if we are not aware of it? How can we enjoy the wonders of the natural world if we remain locked up in our busy minds, away from life? How can we get in touch with the happiness and well-being the natural world brings us if we never get out to experience it? Humans have an amazing capacity to innovate, create and find solutions to problems. We can design more sustainable economic systems, learn to live 'greener' lives, manage nature conservation projects, create nature reserves, reduce our carbon footprints and our usage of water and energy. However, the communal will to take such actions needs to be there first, among as many of us as possible. Once we bring our awareness back to nature and feel a genuine love for the rest of life on the planet, our wonderfully inventive minds will be sure to come up with the necessary innovative solutions to work towards more sustainable living.

Just Love Nature

Who knows if we will save the planet? I am not aiming to turn everyone into a nature conservationist. However, I am sure of one thing: the natural world is an infinite source of wonder and I hope you now have an insight into the potential there is for us all to connect with its infinite beauty. I hope that as you have been reading this book, and through the practice of mindfulness, you have started to notice and enjoy nature a little more in your everyday lives.

The potential for feeling part of the unity of life lies within us all, but it requires time, space and continued practice of mindfulness of the natural world. Don't worry if you don't experience a feeling of deep connection with nature straight away. Just keep noticing and connecting with nature in all the ways we have explored and remain open to anything the natural world has to reveal to you. The more you practise, the more naturally it will come to you. Nevertheless, the development of awareness is a continuous journey of a lifetime. The most important thing is to savour your moments with nature. Enjoy it, have fun with it and cultivate a love for it.

Spend time discovering your favourite ways of appreciating nature. You may enjoy long contemplative walks by yourself through the countryside. You may delight in the adrenalin rush of extreme outdoor sports such as mountain biking, white-water rafting or rock climbing. You might just want to mess around swimming in the sea or making sand castles on a beach. You may seek out encounters with wildlife or spend time bird-watching in nature reserves. You might enjoy the challenge of climbing to the top of mountains or sleeping under the stars. It really doesn't matter *how* you enjoy nature. What matters is to take pleasure in it. Stay aware of how nature calms you, revitalizes you, makes you smile and helps you connect with the here and now of your life.

Be Generous

Once you have discovered your favourite ways of enjoying the natural world, share them with everyone you can. Be generous with your enthusiasm. Inspire other people to explore nature by showing them how amazing it is. Take your family and friends to your favourite natural places. If you have children, take them out into the natural world as often as you can. Let them play in the forests, get dirty jumping in puddles, look after animals, build forts, make little boats out of leaves, catch insects, paddle in streams, throw snowballs and climb trees. You can even join in yourself; these small pleasures are enough to fill us all with a sense of wonder. If you are artistic, express your love of the natural world through your art. Paint it, write about it and photograph it. Celebrate the natural world in every way possible.

I feel at home with nature and, perhaps even more importantly, being in touch with the natural world makes me feel in touch with who I really am. Spending time in nature fills me with a liberating feeling of enjoying being myself, as I let go of any thoughts about who I imagine I should or shouldn't be. As I wander along a beach with the wet sand crunching under my feet, as I stand at the top of a mountain with the wind rushing through my hair, as I lie on my back in the sea looking up at the blue sky above me, I am myself. I love life and I need nothing else in the entire world. In those moments, I am alive, strong and free.

PROTECTING THE LIFE WE LOVE

MINDFULNESS PRACTICE

WAYS TO ENHANCE & SHARE YOUR LOVE OF NATURE

❋

Protecting the natural world starts with cultivating a love of nature. Here are some things you can do:

• Spend time out in the wild and give nature your full attention as often as possible.

• Share your love of nature with your family, friends and colleagues.

• Teach your family and friends some of the mindfulness practices from this book.

• Join a volunteering conservation project or volunteer at your local nature reserve.

• Create a wildlife-friendly garden using guidance from organizations such as the Royal Society for the Protection of Birds.

• Cultivate an attitude of respect and kindness towards animals and plants and avoid harming them deliberately.

• Cultivate appreciation and gratitude for natural resources such as water, air, energy, food. Remember that they are all gifts of nature. Use them sparingly.

• Practise mindfulness of natural sights, scents and sounds as you go through your day.

BIBLIOGRAPHY & WEBSITES

◆

The Web of Life: A New Scientific Understanding of Living Systems by Fritjof Capra
(Anchor Books, New York, 1996)

Lost in the Jungle: A Harrowing True Story of Adventure and Survival by Yossi Ghinsberg
(Skyhorse Publishing, New York, 2009)

The Happiness Trap by Russ Harris (Constable and Robinson Ltd, London, 2008)

Krishnamurti's Journal by Jiddu Krishnamurti (Victor Gollancz Ltd, London, 1987)

A Sand County Almanac (Outdoor Essays & Reflections) by Aldo Leopold
(Ballantine Books, New York, 1986)

Life With Full Attention by Maitreyabandhu
(Windhorse Publications Ltd, Cambridge, UK, 2011)

The Miracle of Mindfulness by Thich Nhat Hanh (Rider, London, 1991)

Survival of the Beautiful: Art, Science and Evolution by David Rothenberg
(Bloomsbury Publishing Plc, London, 2013)

Happiness and How It Happens: Finding Contentment through Mindfulness by Suryacitta "The
Happy Buddha" (Ivy Press, Lewes, 2011)

Walden; Or, Life in the Woods by Henry David Thoreau (Wilder Publications, Radford, 2008)

The Embodied Mind: Cognitive Science and Human Experience by Francisco Varela
(MIT Press, Cambridge, MA, 1993).

The Diversity of Life by Edward O Wilson (Penguin Books, London, 2001).

Websites

The Natural Change Foundation: www.naturalchange.org.uk

Richard Louv: richardlouv.com

Project Wild Thing: www.projectwildthing.com

Foundation for Deep Ecology: www.deepecology.org

Mindfulness: www.mindfulnet.org

Wildmind: www.wildmind.org

The Nature Conservancy: www.nature.org

BirdLife International: www.birdlife.org

The Royal Society for the Protection of Birds: www.rspb.org.uk

The National Trust: www.nationaltrust.org.uk

The Tree of Life: www.tolweb.org/tree

World Land Trust: www.worldlandtrust.org

ACKNOWLEDGEMENTS

This book is built on countless experiences, conversations and discoveries which have enriched my thinking and feelings about the importance of mindfulness and the natural world over the past few years. Many people have been a part of this journey and have fuelled my passion for the natural world and helped me to explore mindfulness that it would be difficult to name them all – but thank you everyone.

Thanks to every member of my family who, as always, provided me with unwavering support, encouragement, love and enthusiasm as I took on the exciting challenge of writing about my passion.

Thanks to all my friends for their invaluable friendship, support and enthusiasm over the past few months. Writing the book wouldn't have been possible without them all. I want to specifically thank those who contributed to the writing of this book by sharing their experiences of the natural world with me, including: Jonathon Dunn, Toby Gibson, Chloe Hardman, Carolina Hazin, Anne Helme, Shaun Hurrell, Bethan John, Helen Lin, Rory McCann, Ben Phalan and David Wege.

I am particularly grateful to David for his endless patience and support for helping me write the mindfulness practices which are an integral part of the book.

Many thanks to Shakya Kumara and all the friends I have made at the Cambridge Buddhist Centre with whom I have continued to discover the happiness and meaning there is to be found in the practice of mindfulness and who have also shared their ideas and provided support.

I will always be grateful to Monica Perdoni for giving me this truly amazing opportunity; and to Tom Kitch and Jenni Davis from Ivy Press for their enthusiasm, support and sensitivity as they worked with me on the final manuscript.

INDEX